South Wales Transport

Alan Townsin and Chris Taylor

The Transport
Publishing Company
128 Pikes Lane
Glossop Derbyshire
Tel: 045.74.61508

Foreword

by David J. R. Bending
Managing Director
The South Wales Transport Co Ltd

This volume sets out to convey something of the lively history of SWT and, through the illustrations, an impression of the variety of vehicles and types of service operated in its 75 years. Indeed the Company's antecedents can be traced unusually far back in time — to the opening of the railway between Swansea and Oystermouth in 1807, believed to be the first public passenger railway in the world. Yet through all the changing circumstances, SWT has shown itself to be adaptable and today, as the principal bus-operating member of the United Welsh Services Ltd group, it is able to operate highly efficiently in a competetive environment, with a work-force in which the team spirit is strong.

© Transport Publishing Company Limited, May 1989

SBN 0 86317 149 4 (Case)
SBN 0 86317 154 0 (Limp)

TITLES IN THIS SERIES

British Bus Systems

Thames Valley
Brighton Hove & District
Northampton
Southdown
Dodds/AA Motor Services
Lancashire United
Liverpool Buses

COMPANION VOLUMES

Best of British Buses

No. 9 Leyland Titans 1945-84
No. 10 Post War Regents
No. 11 Post War Daimlers
British Bus Story
British Bus Story 1950s
British Bus Story 1960s
British Bus Story Early 1970s

In course of preparation

Glasgow Buses
SHMD Joint Board
British Bus Story Late 70s

Illustrated list of all titles available on receipt of SAE

Designed, typeset and produced for the Publishers by Mopok Graphics, 128 Pikes Lane, Glossop, Derbyshire Printed and bound in Great Britain

Contents

Photo Credits

Most of the photographs reproduced in this book have come from Phil. Trotter or the South Wales Transport Company's collection. The remainder have come from the collections of the following and are attributed to the appropriate photographer where known.

Brush (TPC collection; courtesy R. T. Morgan; courtesy M. Sutcliffe) — 12(bottom), 13, 15(top), 21(top two), 23(2nd top), 25(top)
Bus & Coach — 55(bottom)
C. Carter — 65(top left)
A. B. Cross — 31(centre), 32(top), 35(top), 36(bottom), 59(bottom), 65(top right)
J. E. Cull — 22(2nd bottom)
Duple (TPC collection) — 72(top)
R. N. Hannay collection — 45(centre)
J. F. Higham — 10(top), 19(top), 65(centre)
B. A. Jenkins — 60(top right)
Kendon Photos — 73(top)
Leyland Bus (TPC collection; courtesy BCVM) — 11(top, bottom), 19(bottom), 20(top two), 21(bottom), 23(2nd bottom), 26(bottom), 27(bottom), 51(top two), 63(top & bottom)
R. F. Mack (TPC collection) — 37(centre), 47(top & bottom), 53(top), 67(both right), 68(lower right)
R. Marshall — 27(centre), 29(top), 51(bottom right), 61(centre left)
MCW — 20(bottom), 22(centre), 39(top), 43(top)
Maidstone & District & East Kent Bus Club — 10(bottom)
R. A. Mills — 31(bottom)
Photofives — 55(top left), 57(bottom), 52(top), 67(lower left), 69(bottom)

P. J. Relph — 39(bottom), 46(top)
A. Richardson — 42(centre)
C. W. Routh — 61(centre right), 68(lower left)
R. Simpson — 37(bottom)
South Wales Evening Post — 33
South Wales Transport — 6, 7, 11(centre), 15(bottom), 26(top), 28, 29(bottom), 34(top), 35(bottom), 36(top), 37(top), 38(top & bottom), 40, 41, 42(top), 43(bottom), 44(top), 45(top), 46(bottom), 48(top), 54(top), 56(bottom), 57(top), 59(top), 60(bottom), 69(top), 73(bottom), 74(top), 80, 89, 92, 93, 94, 95
South Wales Transport collection — 17(bottom right), 49(top), 68(top)
A. A. Townsin collection — 60(top left)
TPC collection — 47(second top)
C. J. Taylor collection — 8, 9, 10(both upper), 12(top), 14(bottom), 16(bottom), 17(top & left two), 18(lower), 22(top), 23(top & bottom), 24(bottom), 25(bottom), 27(top), 32(bottom), 59(centre), 61(top two), 63(centre two), 64
S. N. J. White — 60(centre)

This view of Ravenhill garage, Swansea, was taken soon after it was completed in 1937. The extra space it provided was soon to be needed for the buses purchased to replace the Swansea Improvements and Tramways Co fleet of trams. Nearest the camera is one of the fleet of 50 AEC Regent petrol-engined double-deckers with Brush bodywork placed in service in 1932 — the same vehicle, WN4760, is also illustrated on page 18. On the left is a 1933 AEC Renown six-wheel single-decker and beyond the Regent, a Dennis Lancet and an AEC Regal Mark II. Various older Dennis E, ES or EV single-deckers are lined-up along the far wall.

Introduction

Superficially, The South Wales Transport Company Limited began life in 1914 as a typical bus-operating subsidiary of the British Electric Traction Company Limited. It was established to provide bus services centred on a town where BET already had a substantial electric tramway undertaking, in this case the Swansea Improvements and Tramways Company, in much the same way as occurred in several other parts of the country. Yet its subsequent history has been far from straightforward.

The retention of the same company title through the subsequent changes of ownership and group organisation underlines the sense of continuity, stability and wealth of experience which are among SWT's key assets 75 years later. Even so, there have been several periods when the Company's future was in doubt.

There were only a few months following the beginning of operation in May 1914 before the outbreak of the 1914-18 war frustrated expansion plans into other parts of South Wales. The post-war years were a period of development, but not for SWT alone. South Wales was a fertile area for the growth of independent bus operators, often having the support of their local communities. Although Swansea Corporation protected the SITC tramway system and, to some degree, SWT by means of the licensing powers local authorities then held, the independents flourished.

The introduction of the road service licensing system laid down in the Road Traffic Act of 1930 often tended to work to the benefit of major company operators. However, SWT had not established the dominance that applied in most other areas, and the security of routes given by the new system also applied to the independents. Its financial position was poor, the Company trading at a substantial loss in 1931, and it is significant that no railway company investment occurred, as applied at that time with most of the major BET or Tilling associated operating companies.

Gradually a process of amalgamation of many of the stronger independents began to occur as such businesses were acquired by the executive directors of the Red & White concern, unable to expand in its own area of south-east Wales.

In 1936-37, buses bearing the South Wales fleetname replaced the Swansea trams, though much of the new fleet was actually owned by SITC, and SWT's own 'trams' on the Swansea and Mumbles Railway were to survive until 1960. Ravenhill depot and the central works adjoining the present headquarters was established but the era of competition was by no means over. United Welsh Services Limited was established in 1939 to amalgamate the Red & White associated companies in the area around Swansea and thus two major operating companies belonging to different groups shared much the same area, a rare occurrence by that time.

World War 2 in 1939-45 brought its own problems, with severe bombing of Swansea. A further process of amalgamation brought the Red & White bus interests, including United Welsh, into the Tilling group, by then State-owned, in 1950, but SWT continued as a BET subsidiary. In general, a period of greater stability ensued, aided by agreements to exchange some routes between SWT and United Welsh in 1939 and again in 1953.

Acquisitions of other operators by SWT were not as numerous as those of some other major companies in areas where there were many independent concerns. However, two significant ones arose from special circumstances. Llanelly District Traction, running trolleybuses and motor buses was, in effect, a left-over from the nationalisation of electricity, including the company of which it was part. Its sale to SWT in 1952 was, at the time, a unique instance of what would now be called privatisation, the trolleybuses soon being replaced. James of Ammanford had been bought by BET in 1950 but the need for rationalisation to cope with falling traffic and rising costs led to it being merged into SWT in 1962.

The purchase of BET's bus interests in Britain on behalf of the State and the formation of the National Bus Company to take over both Tilling and BET bus groups cleared the way for a much bigger merger in 1971. This brought the take-over of United Welsh and two more former BET subsidiaries, Thomas Bros of Port Talbot and Neath & Cardiff, of Neath by SWT. Inflation and difficulty in obtaining approval for fares increases had nearly brought the company to its knees and for some years its

In characteristic south Wales valley surroundings, AEC Renown No. 1240 (303 ECY) is seen en route to Morriston soon after entering service in 1963. One of the first production batch of this model, it had Park Royal bodywork and is representative of the long sequence of AEC double-deckers in SWT's fleet placed in service between 1932 and 1967.

financial position was perilous. The depression of the early 'eighties hit the mining and steel industries and hence called for further service and depot closures.

Yet when a new era of competition began in 1986 as a result of the Transport Act of 1985 which also provided for the privatisation of NBC on the basis of sales of individual companies, SWT proved well able to withstand successive waves of competition under the guidance of the management team which purchased the Company.

The SWT story thus has a remarkable series of twists and turns, as this volume seeks to convey, and that of the vehicles used is no less fascinating. AEC models in remarkable variety formed a major part of the fleet from the 'twenties until the 'seventies — new purchases were exclusively of this make between 1946 and 1962. Yet at different periods there were also substantial numbers of Leyland and Dennis vehicles, while the merger with United Welsh brought in an almost all-Bristol element. The NBC era has left its stamp, but on many routes the Mercedes-Benz minibus is now the most familiar type, and it will be interesting to see how SWT develops in future years.

Alan Townsin   Basingstoke, 1989

Chapter One: A century on the rails

Although The South Wales Transport Co Ltd is celebrating its 75th anniversary, having been registered on 10th February 1914, its antecedents go back over a century earlier. Most of this earlier history related to railways and tramways, but had it not occurred, the pattern of bus operation almost certainly would have been different.

A brochure entitled 'Over 155 Years of Service', issued by the South Wales company at the time of the closing of the Swansea and Mumbles Railway on 5th January 1960, tells how it all began and I can hardly do better than quote from it:-

'Sometime in the year 1800, Sir John Morris, of the Clasemont, began discussing with other influential Swansea citizens the idea of constructing a railway between Swansea Canal and Oystermouth. Probably in secret and with some trepidation. For railroads which were then appearing in other parts of the country were looked upon with a certain amount of suspicion and distaste.

But the Swansea pioneers were undaunted. In 1803 they committed their plan to paper. A year later they promoted a Parliamentary Bill which became law on 19th June of that year. The Act read:

'Whereas the making and maintaining of a Railway or Tramroad for the passage of Wagons and other Carriages to communicate with the Swansea Canal near a certain place called The Brewery Bank, within the Town of Swansea in the County of Glamorgan to, or near to, a certain field called Castle Hill, in the Parish of Oystermouth in the said County of Glamorgan and also the making an maintaining of a Branch of such Railway or Tramroad, to communicate therewith, from a certain place near the Mount in the said Town of Swansea, in the County aforesaid, to, or nearly to, Swansea Pier; and likewise the making and maintaining of another Branch of such Railway or Tramroad to communicate therewith from a certain place near Blackpill, to or nearly to a certain place called Ynys in the Parish of Swansea in the said County of Glamorgan.'

A point of particular interest about this Act is that the 'haling or drawing' of the wagons or other carriages was to be done by 'men, horses or otherwise', powers which were sufficient to cover the introduction of steam locomotives nearly three-quarters of a century later...'

'Originally it was not intended to work the line for passenger traffic, but merely for the purpose of developing the iron mines and limestone quarries. Early documents, however, reveal that passenger traffic first started on 25th March 1807. This service was provided by a contractor who offered the company a fixed sum 'for permission to run a wagon or wagons on the Tramroad for a year . . . for the conveyance of passengers."

This is believed to have been the first public passenger service by rail, either in this country or elsewhere in the world. It was based on horse-drawn traction and hence quite different in character to the Stockton and Darlington Railway but it was nearly 20 years earlier. It was evidently profitable and continued for some years. An account written in 1808 refers to 'a carriage of irregular construction which contains twelve persons and is constructed chiefly of iron, its four wheels run on an iron railway by the aid of one horse, and is an easy and light vehicle'.

Another, dating from 1813, was less complimentary though evidently referring to a different vehicle, being 'a very long carriage, supported on four low iron wheels, carries sixteen persons, exclusive of the driver, is drawn by one horse, and rolls along over an iron rail-road at the rate of five miles an hour, and with the noise of twenty sledgehammers in full play'. This suggests that the joints between the very short lengths of channel-section rail were poorly aligned by that date.

For a while the line prospered, continuing to use horses, though there was an early attempt with sail-power, which must have had its limitations.

'Then in 1826, a road was made between Swansea and Oystermouth. Passengers flocked to the road's horse buses. The railway went out of service for passengers. . . . for nearly thirty years the line lay almost derelict, accommodating only a small quantity of goods traffic. For a time passengers had to rely on road transport between Swansea and Mumbles which was provided by James Williams' Royal Mail omnibuses. The first evidence of

Horse traction was used exclusively from the opening of the Oystermouth Railway to passenger traffic in 1807 until 1877. The lack of any severe gradients made it possible for a single horse to pull what must have been quite a heavy three-compartment carriage with seats on the 'knifeboard' top deck.

This view of Mumbles village shows the pier and railway, with a steam-hauled train of tramway-style carriages as used from around the turn of the century. The pier, and the extension of the railway, had been completed in 1898.

passenger service being resumed by the Railway Company was in the year 1860.

The passenger railway owed its salvation to George Byng Morris who had owned the railway since 1840 under a mortgage foreclosure. He initiated important developments. In 1855, the line was relaid with edge rails and by 1860, a service was opened between Swansea and Oystermouth.

Then for nearly thirty years the affairs of the railway were turbulent. A veritable 'tug-of-war' as to ownership and running rights developed. . . In 1864, while the Blackpill to Swansea section of the Llanelly Railway was under construction, an agreement was reached to sell the Oystermouth Railway for £20,000 to John Dickson, a railway contractor who was interested in extending the Neath and Brecon Railway to the Mumbles. Dickson was unable, however, to pay the amount by the due date. He was adjudicated bankrupt and the Oystermouth Railway remained in the hands of George Byng Morris.'

Meanwhile, interest in street tramways as a means of developing urban public transport was growing. In 1874 the Swansea Improvements and Tramways Co was incorporated by an Act of Parliament. The unusual name reflected its wider role than the operation of horse-drawn tramcars, for it constructed new streets and improved others in the growing town. There was to be a close association with the history of

Swansea and the tramways were operated under leases from Swansea Corporation.

There were implied links between the new Tramways company and the Oystermouth Railway from the beginning, for the leading personality in the formation of the former was Colonel George Grant Francis, who was an associate of George Byng Morris of the latter. The possibilities of linking the two had been forseen and the tramway depot was sited near a junction which would give easy access to the railway.

In 1877, the Swansea Improvements and Tramways Co came to an agreement with Morris to work the Oystermouth railway, paying him an annual rental of £1,600. Within six weeks, steam traction was introduced, a trial trip being made on 16th August 1877, using a Hughes locomotive of the type developed for tramway use, with the mechanism hidden by a tramcar-like superstructure largely on the basis that horses would be less likely to be frightened. This latter point was conceded by the Mayor of Swansea, Dr James Rogers, who had been prominent among a group which opposed the use of steam engines largely because of the danger caused by any horses frightened by them, but his own steed showed no concern when taken near the locomotive. Regular steam services began the following day.

However, John Dickson then reappeared on the scene and, as the result of a court action brought by his

trustees in bankruptcy, the railway had to be put up for auction. Its buyers, for £31,000, proved to be friends of John Dickson and in 1879 the undertaking became the Swansea and Mumbles Railway Co Ltd, with Dickson in charge. The SITC tenancy was repudiated but further legal action allowed the latter the right to work horse-drawn trams immediately behind the Swansea and Mumbles steam trains.

Then, in 1884, Sir John James Jenkins and Robert Capper obtained a lease of the railway and the SITC worked the line by steam for six and a half years, only to lose this position and again be reduced to running horse-drawn cars behind the steam trains for a second time in a period running up to 1896 when horse operation on the railway ceased.

Meanwhile, a new concern, the Mumbles Railway and Pier Company, had been formed in 1889, extending the line from Oystermouth and building a pier at Mumbles. The line was opened in two stages, in 1893 and 1898, the pier also being completed by the latter date.

The latter years of the last century were a time of rapid change in terms of road and street transport. Although steam was to continue to reign supreme on main-line railways for another half-century and more, the steam tramway locomotive was facing a new and powerful competitor in the form of the electric tramcar. In terms of motive power, this effectively moved the steam engine, still the prime mover, to the power station, with electrical energy conveyed to motors (compact enough to fit beneath the tramcar bodywork) by overhead wire via a roof-mounted trolley pole or, latterly in some cases, pantograph or bow collector. More radical still was the motor vehicle with its own petrol engine, then also going through its early development stages.

Electricity was soon accepted as the most effective solution for the tram. The British Electric Traction Co Ltd, registered in London in 1896 by Emile Garcke, was intended from the start to set up electric tramway systems wherever the prospects looked favourable. A controlling interest was acquired in many existing tramway companies, among them being the Swansea Improvements and Tramways Co which came under BET control in 1898.

The Swansea tram system was rapidly converted to electric traction, this work being completed by 1900 and making Swansea the first town in Wales to have electric trams. Negotiations with the two railway companies resulted in the acquisition by the Swansea Improvements and Tramway Company of a lease on the Swansea and Mumbles railway and pier for 999 years.

Oddly enough the application of electric traction on the Mumbles line did not follow immediately, as might have

been expected. A rather imposing design of bogie electric car was produced in 1902, but depended on battery power which proved unsuccessful and the experiment was abandoned the following year, the cars involved being converted to join the fleet of four-wheel tramway style vehicles operated as steam-hauled trains. The locomotives were by that date of conventional saddle or side tank type.

A scheme called the Gower Light Railway had been promoted in 1898, and it was arranged that BET would work this line, which would have connected with the Swansea and Mumbles roughly half-way along its length at Black Pill, continuing westwards along the Gower Peninsular to Port Eynon. However the scheme was dropped and doubtless this reduced the attraction of conversion of the Mumbles line, which continued to be profitable, not least by virtue of its appeal for recreational outings from Swansea.

Meanwhile, motor transport had begun to develop, though it was left to independent operators to make the first moves. A company called Swansea Motor Omnibus Co Ltd was incorporated in January 1899, and services to Sketty and Mumbles began in March and April of that year, among the earliest in the country. Further expansion led to a

proposal for BET to buy the company in 1900. However, the proposal fell through and SMO was wound up, as were many other early ventures using small wagonettes. Had BET gone ahead it might well have been its pioneer venture in motor bus operation.

Several independent operators began motor bus operation in 1909-10. Among them were the brothers George and Rowland Taylor of Llangennith who began to operate Dennis buses into Swansea in 1910, soon adopting the name Vanguard. This was to be one of the sizeable number of businesses which, by a series of amalgamations, can be traced as part of the family tree of South Wales Transport as existing today, although more directly one of the progenitors of United Welsh Services Ltd, which was not taken over by SWT until 1971, and described more fully later.

After electrification of the existing system, the Swansea Improvements and Tramways Co opened new routes and extended existing ones, as well as replacing single-line working by double track in a number of instances. The network served both the docks and many of the residential areas but, as the importance of the town grew, the need for services to surrounding districts increased.

Recent examination of the minutes of the Swansea Improvements and Tramways Co has revealed that, in December 1913, that company ordered ten Leyland 40hp single-deck buses. However, it was reported to the board meeting in February 1914 that the order had been cancelled. The reasons for this can only be a matter for speculation — in 1912 Swansea Corporation had been investigating the possibilities of constructing a tramway to the Mount Pleasant (Townhill) area. Possibly SITC saw buses as a potential answer but clearly the wider scope for running buses led to the formation of South Wales Transport Co Ltd the same month that SITC's order for buses was cancelled, as explained in the next chapter.

The sense of 'occasion' in a trip by motor vehicle in 1910 is nicely conveyed in this view (left) taken in Rhosilly. Rowland Taylor stands by the steering wheel of CY 907, a Dennis with open-sided bodywork. The vehicle shown above, also a Dennis and with partially similar bodywork, differed in having an enclosed compartment at the rear on which was inscribed the fleetname Vanguard adopted by the Taylor brothers; in this case, George is at the wheel. Gower Vanguard Motors, as the firm became, was to be among the many competitors to South Wales Transport until the 1930s.

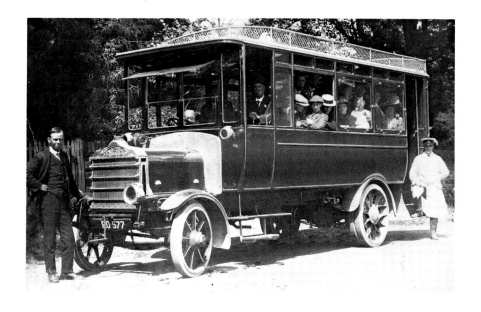

Delays in delivery of the Leyland buses ordered to begin SWT operations led to the hire of vehicles from the other BET subsidiaries during the spring and summer of 1914. Among them was EO 577, this Daimler 40hp model with Brush bodywork from Barrow-in-Furness Tramways.

Chapter Two: The Motor Bus brings competition.

The growing importance of the motor bus had been recognised by BET, which set up a subsidiary to become involved in such activities, originally called the British Automobile Development Co Ltd, in 1905. Renamed British Automobile Traction Co Ltd in 1912, it was by then setting up branches or investing in existing businesses in several parts of the country. However, in places where BET already had substantial tramway interests, motor bus operation was generally put under more direct BET control, and so it was in the Swansea area.

The South Wales Transport Co Ltd was thus set up as a direct BET subsidiary company, though closely linked with the Swansea Improvements and Tramways Co by having the same

management who divided their activities between the two companies. Although it was registered on 10th February 1914, its first service, running from the tram terminus at Ynysforgan to Pontardawe and Ynysmeudwy, did not begin until 2nd May 1914.

The original head office was at the Rutland Street, Swansea, headquarters of SITC, but the buses were housed at premises in Brunswick Street later to be extended and for many years to be the company's headquarters. A garage was also constructed in Fleur-de-Lys, Monmouthshire and one proposed in Merthyr Tydfil. It was intended that SWT would operate throughout South Wales, but hostile attitudes of local councils and wartime shortages caused this to be abandoned, though services were run in

the Merthyr and Caerphilly areas in 1915-17.

Initially, a fleet of fifteen Leyland 40 hp buses was ordered via British Automobile Traction. However, deliveries were delayed, other vehicles being borrowed from elsewhere in the BET group.

In addition, the business of F. L. Lewis of Pontardawe was acquired in the same month, May 1914, as SWT operations began, allowing the route to be extended to Ystalyfera and adding two Milnes-Daimler double-deckers, dating from 1913-14, to the fleet. A horse bus business, owned by Moses Lee and his son James, was also taken over, serving Swansea and Mumbles.

Orders were placed with British Berna, the British builders of chassis to the

The initial choice of SWT was a fleet of Leyland 40hp models, an order for ten placed in February 1914 being quickly followed by five more. Seen here is CY 1517, complete with Brush bodywork — note the roof-mounted headlamps.

Nine British Berna buses were also received, these having chassis built in Newcastle to Swiss design. An order for twelve had been placed in June 1914, but three were cancelled.

The first double-deckers in the SWT fleet were two Milnes-Daimler 30hp models taken over in May 1914 from F. L. Lewis of Pontardawe, this one, L 1128, having entered service with him earlier that year. On the original photograph, it appears that the conductor's cap badge is of the BET magnet-and-wheel style. The chassis was fitted with a lorry body by 1921, surviving until 1929.

Among the collection of less-familiar makes purchased in 1914-15 were five Burford 2-ton models, for which 16-seat seat charabanc bodies by Birch were purchased, including CY 1717. 'South Wales Transport Co Ltd Swansea' was signwritten in full on the rear panel.

design of the Berna concern in Switzerland, for twelve 32.4 hp buses with 32-seat bodywork. Nine of these were delivered and the other cancelled, but hardly had they arrived when the outbreak of the first World War in August 1914 was soon followed by the commandeering of eight Leyland and six Berna chassis. The fleet at the end of the year consisted of seven Leyland, three Berna and the two Milnes-Daimler buses.

A further acquisition in 1915 brought two Karrier and a Napier bus into the fleet from the business of T. E. and J. Evans of Brynseinol, Fforestfach, allowing consolidation of a route to Llanelly. As occurred with other associated companies, orders were placed for eighteen Burford chassis, to most of which bodywork from the vehicles impressed in 1914 was transferred. The shortage of vehicles also promoted the purchase of ten

Signal chassis; five Burford 2-ton models with Birch 16-seat charabanc bodywork were also supplied.

The bodywork of many of these vehicles was transferred again after the war ended in 1918, this time to AEC YC chassis. It was common practice, and legally permissible at that time, to transfer registration numbers with bodywork and this makes the tracing of the identity of early vehicles difficult. The association with AEC thus begun was to continue for half a century, new vehicles of this make being purchased thereafter in most years, apart from a period from around 1928-31 when Dennis vehicles were favoured and the 1939-45 war period, until the mid 'seventies. There were spells during this time when other makes were also added to the fleet, notably Dennis and Leyland in the 'thirties, but South Wales was long regarded as one of AEC's most loyal customers—between 1946 and

1962 no other make of new vehicle was purchased.

A major change in operating conditions for bus services came in 1921, when it was agreed that bus services could be extended from the tram terminus, where they had previously ended, into the centre of Swansea. The trams were protected by a condition imposed by the local authority banning the carriage of passengers on buses for journeys wholly within the borough boundary, an interesting example of municipal protection of a company tram system.

The first forward-control AEC buses in the fleet, delivered in 1922, were four 403-type 54-seat open-top double-deckers with 5.1-litre engines very similar to the S-type then entering service with the London General Omnibus Co Ltd and a further seven similar buses followed in 1923, although twelve more ex-military AEC YC and

In 1921, twelve AEC chassis and eleven bodies were purchased by SWT from the East Kent Road Car Co Ltd, FN 3741 being seen here before transfer. They were quickly re-registered on arrival. It is thought that the East Kent crimson livery and fleetname style may have influenced subsequent South Wales practice.

related models were fitted with bus bodies that year. There was also a major take-over with the purchase of Fairwood Motors Ltd, based in Swansea but operating service to Port Eynon, with eight or more vehicles. The business could be traced back via a series of earlier take-overs to one started by J. Grove of Port Eynon using the name Pioneer in August 1909.

The 1924 new vehicle intake consisted of AEC 503-type chassis basically similar to the 403, but with larger 6.8-litre engines, though still of four-cylinder type, 25 being further open-toppers, the body order being split between Brush and Ransomes, but with a further three similar chassis having charabanc bodies by Strachan and Brown. There was also a newly-registered AEC YB with 32-seat body, but this was the last of the ex-War Department chassis added to the SWT fleet, dating originally from 1918.

Meanwhile, although bus routes were being opened up and extended into the surrounding area, the tramway system was also still growing. The numbers of passengers carried by SI & T trams had exceeded 15 million for every year from 1918 onwards, a figure not reached by SWT buses until 1930, by which date the trams were beginning to decline. The number of bus passengers were growing fast and the distances they covered were usually greater than those on the essentially urban tram system, but in the mid 'twenties, the ratio of numbers carried was still around two to one in favour of the latter. The tram fleet had grown to 60, and was being modernised by the adding of top covers to open-top double-deck cars. New tram bodies were being constructed and experiments on the best type of truck on which to mount them carried out.

The South Wales bus fleet also produced a proportion of its own bodywork from around 1925 to 1932, this generally being mounted on Dennis chassis, largely in favour over that period. Early examples were on the Dennis SOS chassis, normal-control (bonneted) model in the 26-32-seat class, of which eight entered service in 1935 and seven the following year.

Heavier-duty bus orders continued to go to AEC at that stage, there being seven more 503-type buses in 1925, this time with Brush 34-seat single-deck bus

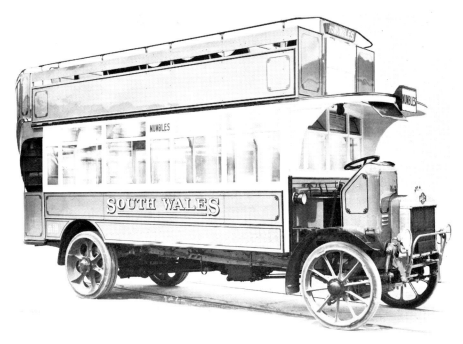

South Wales' first forward-control buses were four AEC double-deckers almost identical to the contemporary S-type models then current in the London General fleet, new in 1922 as shown, and seven generally similar buses followed in 1923. These had 403-type chassis with the 5.1-litre engine, as favoured in London, and bodies built by Fry.

Another of the AEC S-type buses is seen in the mid-to-late 'twenties at St. Helens, Swansea in company with a steam-hauled Swansea and Mumbles train of tramway-style carriages and an SI & T electric tram, all three forms of transport being open-top double-deckers.

The 1924 batch of AEC chassis, though of basically similar S-type design, were 503 models with the larger 6.8-litre engine. Two of the three with Strachan & Brown 32-seat charabanc bodies are seen before delivery, CY 6537 being nearer the camera.

This scene in Brunswick Street garage, Swansea, shows CY 7052, the first of a batch of seven AEC 503-type chassis with Brush 34-seat single-deck bodywork. Alongside are CY 4234 and 4236 two of the AEC YC-type buses first registered in 1921, some of which were re-registered ex-East Kent vehicles.

In 1926, ten of the double-deckers supplied had this pattern of Brush body, with covered top deck. They were on AEC 507 chassis, basically an updated version of the 503 but retaining its straight-framed layout. Thus, although they had what in later years might have been called a lowbridge body layout as illustrated opposite, the overall height of these rather imposing vehicles was littler if any less than a contemporary AEC NS-type bus with conventional body but lower-built chassis. Seen here ready for delivery from Brush with AEC, Walthamstow, trade plates is CY 8686.

bodies. In 1926, thirteen more double-deckers were on the 507 model chassis, mechanically similar to the 503 but with a pressed-steel frame. They were to be the last new vehicles to the delivered to the fleet to have solid tyres. The bodywork on some of them was noteworthy as an early example of a covered-top design with height reduced by the seating layout—the upper deck

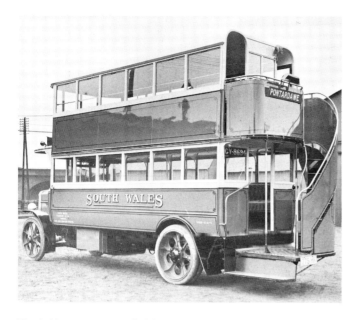

The double-gangway upper-deck layout of the ten covered-top AEC 507 double-deckers of 1926 gave rise to this unusual rear-end design, with an almost tram-like 'balcony' and two doorways, one giving access to each side of the central

back-to-back rows of seats, as shown by CY 8694, also seen at the Brush works in Loughborough. The lower deck ceiling panels had a pronouncedly arched contour.

seats were mounted longitudinally but facing diagonally outwards from the centre-line in a herringbone formation, there being two sunken gangways, one on each side. Brush built ten bodies of this style, the vehicles attracting widespread publicity, though they were to be the last new South Wales double-deckers until 1932.

The SWT fleet has repeatedly offered something out of the ordinary to both the serious transport student and bus enthusiasts in general. A whole family

of special buses was started in 1926 with the first purchased for the Townhill route. Swansea is sometimes compared with Rome in being built on seven hills, and though such comparisons can never be precise, it is certainly a hilly district. As the need for housing for the expanding town increased, the Corporation embarked on a major house-building programme covering the Townhill and nearby Mayhill areas. The route needed to serve them involved a 1½ mile climb almost from sea level to 518ft. The

gradient varied but included quite lengthy stretches of around 1 in 8 and a particularly steep section about half-way up of 1 in 5.6. This was impractical for an electric tram system and extremely severe for the motor vehicles of that period.

The SWT management investigated the possibilities and came to the conclusion that vehicles designed for alpine climbing in Switzerland would be the best proposition then available for the proposed Townhill service.

Swiss experience in building commercial vehicles for hilly districts, doubtless reinforced by the good reputation for quality in general built up by the Saurer concern, led to the choice of this chassis make for the initial Townhill fleet. Brush built the 26-seat bodywork to a design showing the growing styling influence of

the British Electrical Federation (BEF), though also displaying hints of Midland Red ideas in such respects as roof contour and rear-end design. BEF was a BET offshoot providing various services, including bus body design, for associate companies, though some, such as Midland Red, had definite ideas of their own.

Seen tackling part of the Townhill route, CY 8677 was another of the initial fleet of six Saurer buses of 1926. Rear-entrance layout was comparatively unusual on a normal-control vehicle, even though in line with SWT's forward-control models of the period. Engine braking for the descent was enhanced by a variable compression device.

Accordingly, an initial fleet of six Saurer buses was purchased for the inauguration of the service in April 1926. They had a ratchet device to prevent the danger of running back if stalled when climbing, as well as gearing and brake systems well adapted to hilly routes. Brush built 26-seat bus bodywork for them.

The drivers were specially trained both in the correct driving of the type of bus and in negotiating the hill itself. Even so, the public had to be convinced that the service was safe and many free rides were given at the start. Confidence was soon built up and two further Saurer buses were added to the fleet before the end of the year, with a further four in 1930, by which date the service had been augmented to cater for the Mayhill area.

Meanwhile these had been major developments concerning the Swansea and Mumbles line. In 1924, the Swansea Improvements and Tramways Co applied for authority to convert the line to electric traction, an order being granted the following year. In the event, this was not taken up immediately, and in 1927 the lease of the line and the pier at Mumbles was assigned to the South Wales Transport Co Ltd, the stated objective being the co-ordination of Swansea-Mumbles services by road and rail. This might have been taken to imply eventual replacement of the railway by bus services, but this was not to happen for over 30 years.

Instead, the South Wales company itself not only became a 'tramway' operator but was soon to introduce new rolling stock which influenced the thinking of those responsible for fleet renewal in the major British tramway strongholds. Electrification of this line, again with the support of Swansea Corporation, was put in hand, the power being supplied by the Corporation.

In March 1929, the last steam trains ran on the Mumbles Railway and electric traction began. A new fleet of eleven double-deck bogie cars had been built by the Brush concern, and as the line was still officially a light railway, these were generally called railcars in contemporary descriptions. They were much more readily identifiable as very large enclosed electric tramcars, however — indeed, with a 106-seat capacity (58 on the upper deck and 48 downstairs) they were the largest such built for service in Britain, weighing 30 tons each. They could be operated in pairs, the control gear permitting the driver of such a two-car train to control the motors in each bogie, four in all — the electrical equipment was by British Thomson-Houston.

The appearance of the Brush cars, totally enclosed, with domed roof contours and ends which could perhaps be described as a slightly flattened version of the traditional rounded tramcar style, was echoed in subsequent 'advanced' tram designs up to the mid 'thirties. The row of some eleven windows between the interior doors at each end belonged to an earlier age — like earlier Mumbles stock, entrances were provided only on one side — but another modern-looking feature was the use of a pantograph rather than a trolley pole for current collection.

The new cars reduced the journey time for the distance of about 5½ miles from 30 minutes (the steam locomotives had never exceeded 20 mph and averaged more like 7 or 8 mph) to 19 minutes. The number of passengers carried on the line rose from 682,108 in 1925 to 1,192,922 in 1938. Summertime traffic was heavy, with about 60 journeys each way on weekdays — on Bank Holidays up to 40,000 people were carried. The fleet of cars was increased by a further two to a total of 13 in 1930, but this then continued to the end of operation in January 1960.

Meanwhile the bus fleet was passing through a period of concentration on single-deckers. In 1927, twelve ADC 416 models with 32-seat Brush bodywork constituted the only new additions to the fleet. The Associated Daimler Co Ltd had been formed as a joint sales company linking AEC and Daimler and the 416 was a forward-control chassis

Dennis began a period of regular appearance among SWT's vehicle makers in 1925 with an initial batch of eight Dennis SOS model. The vehicle shown was part of the 1926 batch of seven similar chassis, having a 28-seat body by London Lorries of the type with glass side windows and centre gangway but retaining the canvas roof of earlier charabanc designs. The single rear tyres were replaced with twins in 1930 and the vehicle was sold in 1933.

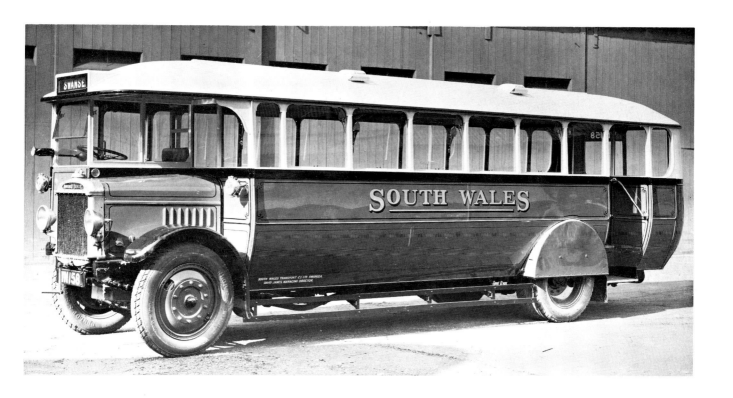

(Above) The batch of twelve ADC single-deckers placed in service in 1927 were of the 416D type, with six-cylinder Daimler engines in the AEC-built 416 chassis. The small-capacity (3½ litre) sleeve-valve engines were troublesome, as often the case elsewhere, but were not replaced as many of the others were. The Brush bodywork showed indications of the evolving BEF style, and may also have influenced subsequent Midland Red practice, for that operator/manufacturer's SOS M type of 1929 had several rather similar body styling features.

(Below) The new fleet of railcars, as they were officially called, built for the newly electrified Swansea & Mumbles Railway in 1929 made an impressive sight, especially when coupled in pairs as seen here. This photograph taken soon after they entered service shows the original livery with much greater use of cream than applied later. The influence of these cars on subsequent British tram design was considerable.

The Dennis E-type first appeared in the fleet in 1928 and examples of this, and the ES and EV models derived from it, continued to be delivered until 1932, building up the largest fleet of the type owned by any operator. Of more orthodox design than the ADC models, they gave generally satisfactory service and this doubtless influenced the purchase of further Dennis single-deckers in the period up to 1939. Bodywork was constructed in SWT's own workshop or, in some cases, rebuilt from that on earlier chassis. The vehicle seen here with a publicity miniature bus of the kind quite often used at the time was an ES model of 1929, WN 1864, one of the first buses to carry a fleet number, in this case 196.

designed and built at the AEC works. The two 423 models added to the SWT fleet the following year were Daimler products, however, and the main intake that year was of Dennis make, twelve of the forward-control E type and seven more of the normal-control SOS type.

The whole of the 1928 and 1929 intake had SWT-built bodywork, generally of 32-seat rear-entrance layout. The 1929 additions to the fleet were all Dennis models of the E family, two being 'plain' E four-cylinder buses followed by 20 of the six-cylinder ES and finally four of the EV type with vacuum as opposed to the previous mechanical brake servo of Rolls Royce design and a radiator of updated design. This Dennis EV model was to remain the South Wales standard choice of single-decker until 1932, there being 20 in 1930, twelve in 1931 and a final six in 1932,

again with bodywork built in the South Wales company's own workshops, although this activity then ceased.

In several respects the period up to around 1931 was the end of an era. Competition between bus operators had become quite intense in the absence of a route licensing system beyond the local systems of individual towns. The whole of south Wales was among the areas of the country where a multiplicity of operators had come into being, the numerous villages and mining communities providing enough business to support small local businesses. Some amalgamations had occurred and a smaller number of concerns had grown into sizeable enterprises.

The South Wales Transport Co Ltd had taken over A. Thomas (MMT Services) of Tirydail near Ammanford, with four-

vehicles in 1927 and in 1928 the Swansea-Bishopston service of The Bishopston and Murton Motors Ltd was taken over jointly by SWT and the Swan Motor Co of Swansea, one of the stronger independent operators which was destined to continue as a separate concern until 1951 and itself part of SWT's family tree, as described later. Six of the Bishopston and Murton fleet passed to SWT, but these two take-overs had little impact on the growth of the business. Some 162 buses were being operated in 1929, by which date the number of passengers carried by SWT had grown to 14 million within the year.

Bearing in mind its longer routes, the bus business had overtaken that of the tramways and hence the South Wales Transport Co Ltd acquired control of the Swansea Improvements and Tramway Co in 1930. This made no appreciable difference to the policy, both concerns continuing to be almost wholly owned by BET and having directors and management in common.

The 'twenties had been a period of intense competition between bus operators in most parts of Britain and there was a widely held view that this was proving unsatisfactory. The Road Traffic Act of 1930 introduced the road service licence system that was to survive until dismantled by the Transport Act of 1985. In effect, established operators were given security of tenure, but south Wales was one of the areas where independent operators continued to survive in large numbers. Most of the larger firms existing in the SWT company's area in 1930 were taken over in due course, usually becoming part of the Red & White group, and hence eventually forming United Welsh. They thus form part of the SWT story as will emerge in later chapters.

The Dennis EV differed most obviously from the E and ES in its more modern style of radiator although it also incorporated changes in mechanical design. Seen here is number 206 (WN 2579) one of the first four supplied to SWT at the end of 1929. The nearside part of the destination box carried an illuminated 'South Wales' display.

The Bishopston and Murton Motors Ltd, of Bishopston, was taken over in July 1928, the six vehicles passing to SWT and including this Leyland RAF-type dating from 1924 and having a Leyland-built body, seen in Singleton Street, Swansea, on the Bishopston service.

(Below) Conversion from solid tyres to pneumatics was common practice in the late 'twenties and early 'thirties. Among SWT vehicles so treated was CY 6372, one of the 1924 batch of AEC 504 double-deckers with bodywork of LGOC S-type design, in this case built by Brush and seen in 1930. It awaits departure on the Port Eynon service.

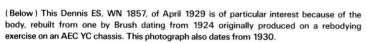

(Below) Local services in Swansea continued to be generally the preserve of the Swansea Improvements & Tramways Co trams, two of which are seen here. The bogie single-decker was quite similar to those operated by the last surviving BET tramway, at Gateshead, one of which is preserved, at Beamish.

(Below) This Dennis ES, WN 1857, of April 1929 is of particular interest because of the body, rebuilt from one by Brush dating from 1924 originally produced on a rebodying exercise on an AEC YC chassis. This photograph also dates from 1930.

In the early 'thirties, South Wales Transport found itself faced with modern fleets of high-quality vehicles run by other operators. An example was this Swan Motor Co Leyland Titan TD1 with 48-seat Leyland body, No. 10 (WN 3645) placed in service in 1931 when SWT had no double-deckers newer than 1926 models — the design of such vehicles had been revolutionised during that interval. Swan ran jointly with SWT on certain routes, surviving until 1952 when it was taken over by United Welsh.

The answer was the purchase by SWT of a new fleet of some 50 double-deckers, a move that must have required courage when the company's finances were poor and the Road Traffic Act of 1930 had not damped down competition in the way that applied elsewhere. The choice of chassis was the AEC Regent with petrol engine as then still standard, on which were mounted Brush bodies of lowbridge type. The first batch of 20 were ordered in the spring of 1932 and No. 260 (WN 4760) is seen in an official Brush photograph before delivery. One reason for the expansion of this order may have been that a first stage of SITC tramway abandonment was to take place in September 1932 when the Morriston to Ynysforgan section was replaced by SWT buses.

Chapter Three: The 'thirties—a period of variety

The Road Traffic Act of 1930 is sometimes said to have created monopoly conditions but at least fifteen operators in addition to South Wales obtained licences to run into Swansea in the aftermath. Indeed, their position was stronger as what had previously sometimes been illegal operation was now licensed. Generally they served towns, villages or areas not covered by SWT, but the main roads into Swansea were often covered by several operators. Gradually they tended to sell

out or amalgamate, most of the prominent ones eventually forming part of the SWT family tree.

Among the more important were Swan Motors of Swansea; D. Bassett and Enterprize, both of Gorseinon (and which amalgamated as Bassett-Enterprise Ltd in 1935); Gower Vanguard; West Wales, of Tycroes, Rees and Williams, also of Tycroes; J. James, of Ammanford; Eclipse, of Clydach; Bluebird of Skewen, and Imperial, of Abercynon. Almost all were buying

modern vehicles and several set high standards.

The financial position of SWT was poor, no dividend having been paid from 1928 and the depression resulted in a loss of £3,875, a sizeable sum in those days, in 1931. The Chairman and Managing Director both retired and under their successors, Sidney Garcke and P. R. Blake respectively, a new regime began. Directors and staff received cuts in salary and some left, but the tight financial position persisted

The second batch of 30 AEC Regent buses delivered towards the end of 1932 had a different style of front-end on otherwise similar Brush bodywork, with slightly more rake to the upper-deck, possibly inspired by the Short Bros design just visible on another Regent belonging to Bassett on the left of this picture. The rounded cab front was another feature then growing in favour. The petrol-engined Regent chassis proved very successful with SWT, though inevitably heavier on fuel than later oil-engined models, but the Brush bodywork required extensive rebuilting after about five years' service. This particular vehicle, 292 (WN 4892) is seen as fitted with a very early example of the AEC 7.7-litre oil engine in December 1934, the 'Oil Engine' radiator badge being visible below the 'Regent' lettering — it performed well but no others were converted, possibly because of the bodywork's limitations. Several were sold in 1938-9 and all had gone by 1946.

and dividends were not resumed until after 1937.

Modernisation of the South Wales fleet took a big step forward in 1932, when a fleet of 50 AEC Regent double-deckers entered service. A TSM (Tilling-Stevens) six-cylinder double-decker demonstrator was also tried, but AEC six-cylinder buses were to play a major part in the company's new vehicle intake for many years. The Regent buses all had Brush 51-seat lowbridge bodywork but were delivered in two batches of 20 and 30 respectively, the second batch having a slightly modified cab design, with curved front dash panel. They were all on the then recently introduced 16ft. 3in. wheelbase chassis and had petrol engines, thought to be the 110mm-bore 7.4-litre unit by then standard.

The 1933 deliveries were also all AEC, but this time single-deck and made up for the smaller numbers in interest. Ten were Regal saloons, with chassis generally equivalent to the previous year's double-deckers but with bodywork to the design of the British Electrical Federation, BET's central organisation co-ordinating vehicle and other supplies, built by Weymann. They were built to a 'luxury saloon' specification with 28 coach seats and could be counted as an early version of

what would later have been regarded as dual purpose vehicles. Two more overtly luxurious vehicles were built on the normal-control (bonneted) Ranger chassis, and had spacious 20-seat folding-roof coach bodies by Harrington.

The remaining five vehicles constituted the second-generation approach to the special needs of the Townhill route, following trials with an AEC demonstrator which had begun in October 1932. They, like the demonstrator, were on AEC Renown six-wheel chassis and the production buses having 40-seat bodywork by Brush. They were fitted with AEC 8.8-litre oil

In October 1932, a new era for the Townhill route, with its steep gradients, began. A special demonstrator had been built by AEC, based on the contemporary six-wheeled Renown in its long-wheelbase 664-model form, registered MV 3711. It was petrol-engined but had the preselective gearbox by then being offered as an option, a sprag brake similar in principle to that on the Saurer buses and a special lightweight body built by Park Royal, originally seating 38 though this was later increased to 40. A batch of AEC Renown buses was ordered for delivery in 1933 and this vehicle was purchased that year, taking the number 316, immediately after those vehicles. Seen here as built, it had a plain underlined version of the fleetname which was obsolete by that date.

In 1933, SWT's additions to the fleet included examples of two more AEC models. Two of the normal-control Ranger chassis with spacious 20-seat Harrington bodywork were delivered in June for use on a new range of seven and fourteen day tours. Somewhat similar vehicles built in 1931 were in use by Devon General, by then also a member of the BET group, originally being built for the Timpson's Grey cars fleet. In both cases almost the whole of the roof folded. This picture of number 299 (WN 5399) is reproduced from an AEC advertisement — the vehicle survived until 1949.

A second AEC demonstrator was prepared for SWT's needs receiving the registration AMD 48 in the spring of 1933 — three-letter marks were only just appearing at the time. This time it was a conventional two-axle forward-control Regal chassis, but with the AEC 8.8-litre oil engine being fitted to a growing share of production — the forward-mounted radiator is evident in this view. The preselective gearbox and sprag gear were again specified, indicating that Townhill was in mind but this time with the oil engine as the main item of interest. The body was again by Park Royal, at whose works it is seen, with 32 seats in this case, and this vehicle was also purchased, becoming number 317.

(diesel) engines, and were SWT's first oil-engined buses — this unit having been fitted to another demonstrator, in this case a Regal, the Renown demonstrator having been petrol from new — both were also purchased by SWT. The Renown buses also had fluid flywheels and preselective gearboxes, doubtless chosen partly on the grounds that such units could be relied upon to give a positive gear-change, eliminating the risk of a missed gear and possible runaway should the brakes prove unable to cope with the consequent lack of engine braking. Similar transmission was long to be a Townhill speciality — elsewhere, SWT generally continued to favour the conventional 'crash' (or to be more precise, constant-mesh third gear) unit.

In 1934, there was a reversion to Dennis, when twelve of the Lancet single-deck chassis were purchased. This had a four-cylinder petrol engine very like that of the E and EV, so many of its characteristics were already well

The largest batch of vehicles taken into stock by SWT in 1933 was that of ten AEC Regal models with Weymann 28-seat bodywork officially described as of luxury saloon type. These were petrol-engined, doubtless in the interest of the smoother and quieter running. The bodywork was to the contemporary 'Federation' outline, more usually associated with Leyland chassis though to be found on quite a range of chassis makes then being supplied to many, though by no means all, companies associated with BET. Number 301 (WN 5401), the first of the batch, is seen when new — all ten were impressed for service with the Royal Air Force in July 1940 and no less than six were lost by enemy action, including this one.

The pair of AEC demonstrators were followed by a batch of five Townhill vehicles combining some of their features. They were AEC Renown six-wheelers, this time with 8.8-litre oil engines as well as preselective gearboxes, and were thus the first SWT diesel buses purchased. Brush built the 40-seat rear-entrance bodywork to a rather nondescript style rather than the distinctive Federation style that might have been expected. Number 315 (WN5815) is seen in these Brush official pictures dated July 1933.

(Below) Among the staff who left when cuts in salary followed SWT's loss-making period in 1931 was S. C. Kenwood, the chief traffic inspector who had been with the company since 1914. He started his own business, Swansea Bus Services Ltd, in 1932, running to Morriston, and his name appears as Managing Director on this 1933 Leyland Lion LT5 with Leyland body. Unfortunately the effort is said to have killed him and the company was purchased by the Swan concern.

known in the fleet. Weymann received the body contract for these and eight AEC Renown double-deckers, though the latter, on the long-wheelbase chassis and thus 30ft. long, had metal-framed 64-seat bodywork. They had 8.8-litre oil engines and preselective gearboxes, being used on the Swansea-Llanelly service in partnership with Bassett's AEC Renown buses.

Yet more variety was evident in 1935, though all deliveries that year were single-deck. Some had entrance doors just behind the front axle—previously SWT had favoured the rear entrance for single-deckers. In addition to a dozen more Dennis Lancet buses with Weymann 32-seat bodywork, there were three types of single-decker not previously seen in the fleet. Five were on Daimler COG5 chassis with Weymann 35-seat bodywork, for the Townhill route. The Gardner 5LW engine of this model was not very powerful but the preselective gearbox specified was of the five-speed type—still quite a rare feature at that date and, in addition, the rear axle ratio was 7.0 to 1. This latter implied a top speed of about 28 mph, quite adequate for the route and doubtless giving good climb capability, even though any level road running must have been tedious.

Also used on Townhill were five of the revolutionary AEC Q side-engined model, again following the running of a demonstrator of the same type, also acquired. The Q-type was a very advanced design for its day, with the engine mounted just behind the offside front wheel and driving the rear axle via fluid flywheel and preselective gearbox. They had the 7.7-litre AEC oil engine originally designed for this model, although they were not quite the first buses so powered in the fleet. One of the 1932 batch of Regents had been converted with an early example of the 7.7 engine as redesigned for conventional chassis in December

A return to Dennis as supplier of single-deck chassis was made in March 1934, when a dozen of the Lancet model were supplied. Mechanically simple, and quite economical by petrol engine standards, the Lancet must have had a strong appeal to a company struggling to improve its financial position because of its modest cost. They were described as proving quite satisfactory by the General Manager in his subsequent reports to the Directors. Weymann built the 32-seat bodywork to a style with well-rounded rear panels — the first vehicle, 318 (WN 6218) is seen here. Five went to the War Department in 1940, but most of the rest were withdrawn in 1948.

The other vehicles delivered in March 1934 contrasted in almost all respects to the unpretentious and modest-sized Lancets. A fleet of eight AEC Renown six-wheel double-deckers was purchased for the Llanelly-Swansea service to operate jointly with three run by Bassett. It is a remarkable fact that two-thirds of the production of the Renown long-wheelbase model during the 1932-34 period went to the South Wales area; this SWT batch had 8.8-litre engines, preselective transmission and Weymann metal-framed bodywork, incorporating the MCW patented construction originally developed by Metro-Cammell. Although of generally sound and substantial design, these buses, and the Townhill Renowns, were not free from troubles in their early years — SWT's operating conditions were tough, with hilly terrain and the various new AEC designs were apt to receive a baptism of fire there. In the case of the double-deck Renowns, the preselective gearboxes, among the last for AEC of Daimler manufacture, proved inadequate and were replaced by AEC-built units. These buses, still modern-looking but doubtless quite expensive to operate, were withdrawn in 1948-49.

Another approach to the Townhill route problem came in February-March 1935 when, after trials with a demonstrator (ADU 469), five Daimler COG5 single-deckers were delivered. These had Weymann metal-framed 35-seat bodywork and compensated for the modest power of their five-cylinder Gardner engines by suitable gearing. The result was very successful, as the vehicles proved both reliable and economical. However, no more were purchased, possibly because they were relatively expensive as compared to the heavily discounted cost of AEC or Leyland buses negotiated by BET. In this case the demonstrator, ADU 469, with Willowbrook body seen below on the Townhill route, was not purchased — it was later sold to the Farsley Omnibus Co Leeds.

1934. The South Wales examples all had 39-seat bodywork, that on the demonstrator being by Weymann and the production buses by Brush.

As if that was not enough in terms of variety, the 1935 delivery of 'luxury saloons' consisted of six Leyland Tiger TS7 chassis with the smooth-running 8.6-litre oil engine and Weymann Federation-type 28-seat bodywork. These were the first new Leyland vehicles since 1914 for the SWT fleet — although AEC was to remain dominant for most of the period up to the early 'seventies, Leyland was to be a major supplier in the late 'thirties.

The 1936 deliveries included the last batch of petrol-engined buses

The sheer variety of the SWT single-deck intake in the 'thirties seems amazing in retrospect. The AEC Q side-engined model was one of the most revolutionary on the British market at the time but had got off to a very slow start after its introduction in 1932. Interest perked up a little after the introduction of the oil-engined version in 1933, yet the demonstrator BML 488 built in 1934 and supplied for trial use by SWT was the first sign of interest by a company belonging to one of the major groups. It had Weymann bodywork of a style broadly conforming to the Q characteristics as indicated in AEC drawings but with a rear end having affinity to SWT's contemporary Dennis Lancet buses. It was acquired in May 1935 and took the fleet number 365 immediately after the batch of Q buses it inspired.

An order for five Q-type buses was placed and delivered in 1935, Brush being given the body contract. They were based on a 1933 AEC body outline drawing to which previous examples had been built by Duple and Weymann, slightly 'toned down' from the more coach-like original concept. The first, number 360, delivered in June had a sliding entrance door but the remainder, dating from November, had inset open entrance doorways, the seating capacity being 39 in all five, as on the demonstrator. Number 361 (WN 8261) is seen, right and is nearest the camera in the pre-delivery line-up at AEC's works seen below. They were purchased for the Townhill service and although the specification (allowing almost as many seats as the Renowns in a more compact bus having fluid flywheel preselective transmission as standard) fitted the need well in some ways, the model could be marginal on cooling even in less arduous conditions. No more were purchased and they were withdrawn in 1949.

Both more orthodox and more successful were six Leyland Tiger TS7 oil-engined models with a mildly updated version of the 28-seat luxury saloon bodywork fitted to the 1933 AEC Regal batch, again built by Weymann to Federation design. Apart from two taken by the War Department in 1940, they proved the longest-lasting of all SWT's 1935 intake, three remaining in service until 1955, albeit with bodywork extensively rebuilt. They were purchased for summer excursion or hire and winter stage services in hilly districts.

Delivery of Dennis Lancet buses continued steadily, the last dozen of the 'Mark I' variety arriving in 1936, and constituting the last new petrol-engined buses purchased by SWT. Weymann again built the timber-framed bodywork, which incorporated quite well rounded rear panels though the oval rear window gave a more old-fashioned look than conveyed by this view of 376 (WN 8976). The whole batch was taken by the War Department in 1940, none returning to SWT though most saw further civilian service — this particular one found its way into the fleet of Rowbotham of Harriseahead, Stoke where it received a Gardner engine and new Lawton body, surviving until 1958.

The good results from the 1935 Leyland Tiger models doubtless led to the purchase of Leyland Titan TD4 chassis for the six lowbridge double-deckers purchased early in 1936. The Weymann metal-framed lowbridge bodies were also of a well-proved design, though the 55-seat capacity, with 29 upstairs, was unusual and was cut back to the more usual 27 up, 26 down on subsequent generally similar bodies. The first bus, number 384 (WN 8984) is seen before delivery from Weymann's — like the others, it remained in service until 1950.

purchased, another dozen Dennis Lancet models with Weymann 32-seat bodywork. Further Leylands arrived in the form of six oil-engined Titan TD4 models, the double-deck equivalent of the TS7, with Weymann metal-framed 55-seat lowbridge bodies, a combination clearly judged very successful, for it was soon to be repeated in mildly updated form.

The AEC contribution consisted of yet another different type, the Regal Mark II model 0862, with 6.6-litre engine, rather than the 7.7-litre unit then normal in the standard Regal of type 0662. There were eight in the batch, which had preselective gearboxes, not a

general option on this model, reputedly of Daimler make—such units had been used on early AEC fluid flywheel buses but from 1934 AEC had built its own version. The 6.6-litre engine was none too successful and 7.7-litre units were fitted to these buses in 1945-46, a process that called for some ingenuity as the 6.6 was a very compact unit, allowing the Brush bodywork, built to what might be called a modified Federation style, to seat 39.

The 1935-7 period was a period of renewed activity in terms of acquisitions by SWT of smaller operators, after quite a long period of inactivity when many other territorial

companies had been particularly busy in this respect. None of the concerns taken over was large—the number of vehicles involved only reached double figures and the total from the seven acquisition was under 50, many being old or completely non-standard and rapidly sold off, some without entering service. There were some notable exceptions, however. The Red & White groups involvement in the Swansea and surrounding areas, fostered by restrictions on its expansion in south east Wales due to company agreements, was causing SWT much concern. It also meant that prices for businesses taken over were high.

Willmore Motors Ltd, of Neath, was acquired by SWT in November 1935 and this 1934 TS6c model, originally with torque converter transmission, was one of the two Leyland Tiger buses taken into SWT stock. Registered TG 8179 it had Massey bodywork — at the time Leyland's own bodybuilding department was being reorganised to switch to metal-framed bodies and Massey was chosen for what would otherwise more probably have been Leyland products in this and other cases.

Two businesses were taken over in May 1935. That of J.M. Bacus & Co of Burry Port, brought from Leyland Lion LT-type buses dating from 1929-30 and a 1932 Leyland Tiger TS4 into the SWT fleet but all were sold by 1938. There were also two AEC Y-type buses, the chassis of one dating back to 1917 — such an age was by then generally regarded as far beyond acceptable limits, and they were not taken into stock. The Gwedraeth Transport Co (1933) Ltd, of Pontyates, contributed ten vehicles, mainly Dennis E of 1926-28, but none were taken into stock. These two firms ran services in the Llanelly-Carmarthen

direction, their purchase strengthening SWT's position in the western end of its territory.

Eastwards, Willmore Motors Ltd of Neath was taken over in November 1935, with five Leyland buses, the two most recent Tiger models of 1934-5 being taken into stock while the remainder, Lion types of 1927-31, were sold immediately. The next acquisition, Treharne Bros of Ponthenry, came in July 1936, but the three vehicles were not taken into stock, despite one being a 1930 AEC Regal.

A more substantial purchase was John Brothers, of Grovesend, Swansea, all of the eleven vehicles purchased being

Adding to SWT's unique and all but complete collection of the AEC passenger models of the 'thirties were eight of the Regal Mark II, introduced as a lighter alternative to the standard Regal. The short bonnet allowed space for 39 seats in the body built by Brush to a modified Federation style — the front end styling had much in common with some Regal II Brush buses built around the same period of mid-1936 for the Northern General Transport fleet. The most unusual feature was the incorporation of preselective gearboxes, and the fact that these were reported to be Daimler-built units strongly suggests that they may have been the units removed from the SWT AEC Renown double-deckers of 1934. They received 7.7-litre direct injection engines in 1945-46 but even so were withdrawn in 1949-50.

After the Tilling-Stevens concern lost its connection with the Tilling group of operating companies and was renamed TS Motors in 1930, quite a vigorous attempt had been made to rebuild volume orders. Demonstrators were sent to various potential operators including several E60A6 six-cylinder double-deckers, one of which, KJ 2915, ran for SWT via TSM's local dealer, Jeffreys of Swansea. It wasn't purchased, passing to the Swan fleet, but in 1936 two similar buses were taken over with the business of John Bros of Grovesend. Seen here is DH 9043, built in similar manner for service with Walsall Corporation in 1931 but purchased by John's in 1932 — it became SWT 407. The 53-seat forward entrance body was by Beadle. One of SWT's AEC Regent buses of 1932 can be seen behind.

taken into stock, despite several being quite old or non-standard to SWT. One, a Leyland Tiger TS7C with Beadle coach body, was virtually new and survived until 1955, though the torque convertor transmission implied by the 'C' in the designation was later replaced by a standard four-speed gearbox. There were two TSM E60A6 double-deckers of the type demonstrated to, but rejected by, SWT in 1932, and a 1935 TSM J5LA7 with Gardner 5LW engine, the last-mentioned being another considerable survivor remaining in SWT service until 1949—all these had Beadle bodywork. Three Leyland Tiger TS3 and one Lion LT1 dated from 1930-31 and the oldest vehicles were three ADC of types 416 and 426 of 1928-9. Their fleet operated routes linking Neath to Llanelly and Llanelly to Porthcawl, the latter being an express service.

A curious purchase was that of three small Thornycroft vehicles previously operated by D. J. Thomas of Maesteg in March 1937 but these were used purely to train ex-tram drivers. However, T. Davies' Osborne Services, of Neath, acquired in June of that year, ran services in the Neath area and four of the seven

vehicles purchased were retained. The two most modern were AEC Q-type 39-seat coaches, a 1934 Weymann-bodied example purchased in 1936 having originally been owned by J. Bullock & Sons of Wakefield, this being converted from petrol to oil just before entering service with SWT; the other, a 1936 Duple-bodied example, was oil-engined from new. Two AEC Regal buses dating from 1930-31 were also retained, but all four had relatively short lives with SWT, possibly due to war circumstances.

Meanwhile, major changes were afoot in Swansea itself. The tramway system had continued to play a major role in the provision of local transport, with the numbers of passengers carried annually dipping only marginally below the 15 million mark in the 1932-36 period. The Swansea Improvements and Tramways Co had a mixed fleet, mainly four-wheel double-deckers but including some bogie cars, which was kept in good condition, but the whole concept of the street tramway was becoming regarded as obsolescent. Operating speeds were low, trams impeding the flow of other traffic, especially in the narrower streets.

In 1935, the tramways company decided to seek parliamentary powers to abandon its system and substitute bus services. The routes were still leased from Swansea Corporation, whose approval had also to be sought. The result was The Swansea and District Transport Act, 1936, which gave power for the Swansea Improvements and Tramways Co to operate bus services in the County Borough of Swansea for 21 years. An annual fee was payable to the Corporation and at the end of that period the Corporation would have power to compulsorily acquire all local services (not merely the former tram routes) on terms set out in the Act. A Transport Advisory Committee with municipal and company members was also set up.

The changeover to buses began in 1936, when routes to the north of the town were converted, the western and eastern areas following in 1937. The tram depot was inadequate to house the newly enlarged bus fleet, so land was purchased at Ravenhill to the north of the town and a 130-vehicle garage completed in 1937, being enlarged two years later by the addition of central workshops.

The fleet of 62 AEC Regent double-deckers purchased for the Swansea tram replacement were early examples of what was to become a familiar specification — 7.7-litre direct-injection A173 engine, 'crash' gearbox and steel-framed Weymann body. This was to apply not only with the South Wales and several other BET fleets but also a variety of other operators until the early post-war period. The first 50 entered service in March 1937 and although not the first with A173 units formed possibly the first big fleet in one location.

In retrospect, it is surprising to discover from the General Manager's reports that the engines gave considerable trouble at first with bearing failures, and fractured crankcases among other problems. AEC was criticised for a series of models which had proved troublesome, and it seems that SWT's tough operating conditions were acting as a proving ground perhaps because too many new designs were being introduced in a brief time. Clearly matters were soon rectified and half the batch lasted 20 years or more, albeit with some extensive body overhauls in SWT shops.

The top and bottom pictures show the special fleetname, omitting the 'Transport Co Ltd' wording and with sans serif lettering, originally used on these buses because of their Swansea Tramways & Improvements Co ownership. Number 8 (ACY 8) is seen (top) ready for delivery from Weymann's while at the foot of the page No. 51 (AWN 551), the first of the second delivery of twelve vehicles to the same design is seen at AEC's works before entering service in July 1937. The centre picture shows ACY 22, renumbered 233 in 1939, as running in its later years, with sliding windows, simplified livery omitting the upper cream band, no louvres in the between-decks panelling but basically looking very much as originally built — it was one of those to complete over 20 years' service.

The interior of the 1937 AEC Regent buses was quite plain in character, though neatly finished. As usual on Weymann double-deck bodies of the period, the front bulkhead windows had quite a high sill level, impeding forward vision for all but tall passengers.

The largest batch of buses bought for the tram replacement comprised 50 AEC Regent models with Weymann 56-seat highbridge bodywork to a new variant of that bodybuilder's metal-framed style, with a curved front-end profile in place of the previous straight slope, though retaining the projecting cab front characteristic of Weymann styles of the mid 'thirties. The chassis had the direct-injection version of the 7.7-litre engine then recently introduced and, indeed, not announced publicly

until 1939, but favoured by several BET companies as well as various other regular AEC customers as soon as it became available. They dated from March 1937 and were numbered from 1 upwards, with matching registration numbers beginning at ACY 1. A further dozen similar buses followed in July, though only the last two digits of the registration numbers matched the fleet numbers, as had been standard practice since 1932. All these vehicles carried South Wales fleet names but also carried

legal lettering to the effect that they were owned by the Swansea Improvements & Tramways Co. This fleet of AEC Regent buses dating from 1937 gave lengthy service—although the first four were withdrawn in 1949, 25 of them lasted until 1957 or later, the last one (ACY 29) remaining until 1959 and then being retained as a training bus until 1960. Another, ACY 9, lasted as a tree-lopper until 1961.

The use of centre-gangway highbridge bodywork for the tram replacement Swansea services was a logical step, for the lowbridge style of body, with side-gangway upper deck, was far from ideal for town service, though later double-deck intake was not necessarily of the 'town highbridge, country lowbridge' pattern that might have been expected. The geography of South Wales, coupled to the spread of mining and other industry, with the railways which largely provided transport for them, meant that bridges crossed many roads and headroom underneath many was limited. Significantly, SWT continued to favour conventional 'crash' gearboxes for its main Swansea and general-purpose fleet. The fluid flywheel and preselective gearbox combination was regarded as a Townhill requirement.

The remainder of the 1937 deliveries consisted of twelve single-deckers, once again Dennis, but of the Lancet II type, with the much more compact front-end and having the Dennis O4 four-cylinder oil engine. South Wales had decided on a maximum seating capacity policy for all its single-deck bus deliveries in the late 'thirties and hence these were 39-seat vehicles, taking advantage of the short bonnet, as had also applied to the previous year's Regal Mark II buses. The bodywork on the 1937 Lancet II buses was by English Electric, a concern that was taking in appreciable share of BET group bus body orders at the time. The style was rather upright in character, the Clayton destination box characteristic of many BET fleets at the time and standard on SWT buses projecting sharply above the roof line in this case.

The 1938 deliveries were purely Leyland and Dennis. The Leylands comprised a total of 61 lowbridge 53-seat double-deckers with Weymann metal-framed bodywork on the Titan TD5 chassis by then current-very like the TD4 in most respects, and with body styling basically like the 1936 batch, but with a slightly curved frontal profile somewhat similar to that of the 1937 Regent batch. The first twelve were legally owned by the Swansea Improvements and Tramways Co, though forming part of a fleet and registration number series of 36 buses delivered between February and May 1938. A subsequent batch of 25 followed almost immediately in June-July.

Between the two series of TD5 models came eleven Dennis Lancet II,

The last of the batch to remain in service was ACY 29, seen here still looking smart when photographed in York Street, Swansea, on learner duties. It was withdrawn from passenger service in 1959 and continued as a training bus until 1960. It might have been regarded as a prime candidate for preservation had it survived a little longer.

The Dennis Lancet II, with Dennis 04 oil engine, was SWT's main choice of single-decker in 1937-39. The first batch, dating from May-July 1937, comprised twelve chassis with 39-seat bus bodies by English Electric, number 64 (AWN 564) being seen here when new. All were withdrawn in 1949 and scrapped.

Double-deck deliveries in 1938-39 were entirely Leyland Titan TD5 models with Weymann lowbridge bodywork. This example from the second 1938 delivery, photographed in Caer Street, Gigea, heading for Brynmill, was originally No. 127 but had become 544 in the 1939 re-numbering, being seen after post-war major overhaul. These buses were well liked and gave good service, if not quite so lengthy as the Regents; this one remaining in service until 1953.

again with O4 engines but this time with Dennis 32-seat coach bodywork and having five-speed overdrive gearboxes. They were delivered between April and July 1938, the last one being noteworthy as it was not on a new chassis but one that had been supplied to the Birmingham & Midland Motor Omnibus Co Ltd (Midland Red) the previous year, having entered service with a 1934 body, built by Short Bros to Midland Red design, in July 1937, registered DHA 200. However it was operated only for a few months before the body was removed and the chassis sold to South Wales in December 1937, being put on one side and then sent for bodying with the new chassis, with only its Smethwick registration number, so characteristic of BMMO, to reveal its origin. In those days, BMMO used its own make of chassis exclusively and it had never been likely that the vehicle would be any more than an experimental exercise. At that date, Dennis produced a sizeable proportion of the coach bodywork fitted to Lancet chassis, but more usually for

independent operators — these particular vehicles had curved-glass cantrail windows as well as sliding roofs. They were delivered in the crimson and cream livery but in October, it was decided to repaint them cream and black, perhaps to combat the impact of independent operators' coaches, usually painted in light-coloured liveries by that date. This continued until renovated in 1947-8 when they reverted to a crimson livery.

In 1939, two further batches of AEC Renown six-wheel single-deckers for the Townhill service appeared, of seven and six vehicles respectively, though in fact they all entered service in May of that year. They had 8.8-litre engines, as on the previous Renowns, but this time of direct-injection type, and are believed to have had fluid flywheels and preselective transmission. Official records quote that both rear axles were driven, but this was standard on all variants of the model. They had 39-seat bodywork by Brush to a style with some affinity to the BET Federation design of the period as far as the front-end was

concerned but with rather more curvacious rear-end treatment. They survived until the early 'fifties, by which time photographs suggest that some may have received 7.7-litre engines.

Once again there were the almost customary dozen Dennis Lancet single-deckers, more of the O4-engined Mark II variety, this time with 39-seat bodywork by Weymann to a rather similar style to that of the Renown with which they were almost exactly contemporary, being delivered in April-May 1939.

A further 25 Weymann lowbridge bodied Leyland Titans completed the 1939 deliveries, and were in fact the first to arrive, dating from March. They were virtually identical to the 1938 batch in both chassis and body design, and it has become clear that they were again TD5 models, even though some post-war South Wales records quoted them as TD7. This latter model was not put into production until the end of 1939 and differed in several visual respects which would have been clearly evident on photographs.

At that point, deliveries of new

It was significant that after the variety of specifications for Townhill buses that had been tried in the mid 'thirties, the vehicles delivered for use on this route in 1939 returned to the 1933 concept — AEC Renown six-wheelers with 8.8-litre engines. They seated 39, no more than the Q or Regal Mark II or, for that matter, the Dennis Lancet II buses being favoured by SWT for use elsewhere at that time. However, the extra 2ft. 6in. of length (3ft. overall) permitted under the regulations of the time when three axles were provided allowed for more spacious seating, valuable on a busy town route, as well as a few extra inches for an engine man enough for the job.

The AEC 8.8-litre engine, generally superseded by the '7.7' from 1935, had remained in production and was still being specified by several operators with hilly routes, such as Sheffield, Halifax and Brighton Corporation, and was also now available in more economical direct injection form. No official photographs of these vehicles when new seem to have survived but this view of CWN 395, by then numbered 43, indicates the original condition. The engine installation appears to have been similar to that on the London Transport 10T10 Green Line coaches built the previous year, with only a slight forward projection of the radiator beyond the position used with the 7.7-litre engine.

By 1950, pre-war vehicles had often swapped units in the course of overhaul and CCY 951, originally numbered 151 when delivered in May 1939 but renumbered 36 later that year, is seen in Castle Street, Swansea with the shorter radiator bearing the 'Oil Engine' lettering as used on SWT's 1933 and 1934 AEC Renown buses. The Brush bodywork, at this stage at least, had sliding windows rather than the half-drops evident on CWN 395. The styling had a touch of 'Federation' flavour, particularly around the front end, but the build was higher and the rear of the body more curvaceous. These are still believed to have been the last six-wheel single-deck motor buses with a double-drive rear bogie to enter service in Britain.

This view of number 45, originally 197 (CWN 397) shows a further stage of development. The radiator is again of the short variety as used by AEC up to 1937 but, more significantly, it has moved back, with the front face virtually flush with the cab front. It is also set slightly lower and the bonnet side appears to be of the post-war type as used on the Regent II. It seems virtually certain that a 7.7-litre engine had been fitted — doubtless there were surplus units available from scrapped Regents, and as the buses were being used on routes other than Townhill, the loss of power would not have mattered greatly. Originally, a small route number box had been fitted over the first nearside window bay but this had been removed. Withdrawals began in 1951, but most of these interesting buses ran until 1954-55.

The 1939 batch of double-deckers comprised 25 further Leyland Titan TD5 chassis with Weymann lowbridge bodywork, virtually identical to the 1938 deliveries. South Wales' then normal practice of matching the last two digits of registration and fleet numbers was followed when they were delivered, CCY 978 being originally fleet number 178 when new in March 1939 but later in that year it became number 579, being seen in Oxford Street as such in 1950, with a 1946 AEC Regent, number 277 (DWN 654) in pursuit — it was withdrawn in 1953. The renumbering of this particular batch was particularly confused, for although 170-194 became 568-592, they were almost all out of order. The erroneous description of these buses in some records as TD7 models may have been due to an order for twelve Leyland double-deckers placed in July 1939, but not fulfilled — they would doubtless have been of this type.

The last dozen Dennis Lancet II models received Weymann 39-seat bodywork of a style quite like that of the AEC Renown buses of the same year. Number 160 (CCY 960) is seen ready for delivery from the bodybuilders on a gloomy day in the spring of 1939. The complete batch was withdrawn in 1949, giving a ten-year life span, regarded as relatively long when they were built but decidedly short by 1949 standards when production of new vehicles was still far from meeting the demand.

vehicles to SWT ceased until after the 1939-45 war — remarkably no wartime buses of any kind were supplied. There had also been no further additions to the fleet resulting from acquisitions in the 1938-39 period. There had been a take-over of two services in September 1938 from Gorseinon and District Omnibus Services, together with five vehicles of unknown identity, but they were not taken into stock. This operator had been acquired jointly with the Red & White organisation. By that date, Red & White had acquired several operators in the area round Swansea and although some had continued to run for a time under their own names, it was decided to create a new subsidiary company, United Welsh Services Ltd. In March 1939, in a deal relating to services to Cefneithin, one 1928 Dennis E been acquired by SWT from United Welsh, but it was not taken into stock.

In the latter part of 1939, the SWT fleet was renumbered. In place of what was

effectively a single system which had reached 410 in 1935 and then reverted to 1 in 1937, reaching 200 by 1939, a new classified system was introduced. The vehicles actually involved in the renumbering can be summarised thus under their new members:

1-48 AEC single-deck	total 48
51-58 AEC Renown double-deck	total 8
201-263 AEC Regent oil	total 63
301-325 AEC Regent petrol	total 25
401-405 Daimler single-deck	total 5
451 TSM single-deck	total 1
501-592 Leyland double-deck	total 92
701-709 Leyland single-deck	total 9
801-836 Dennis Lancet petrol	total 36
851-885 Dennis Lancet oil	total 35
	Grand total 322

The scheme had some obvious logical merit, and clearly numbering the petrol Regents, soon due for withdrawal, 301 up allowed further oil-engined examples to spread upward into this

range, as indeed happened after the war. On the other hand, making the one Regent converted from petrol to oil 201 meant that the vehicles registered ACY1-50 became 202-51, which seemed like a recipe for confusion, and the partial matching of fleet and registration numbers was largely lost. Within the AEC single-deckers, the Renown six-wheeler became 30-48.

More important, South Wales entered the war period with a modern fleet, especially of double-deckers, with 154 vehicles on efficient and reliable direct-injection Leyland and AEC chassis with durable metal-framed Weymann bodywork, most of them barely more than two years old. By the end of the war, that had extended, by almost six years, of course, quite apart from the inevitable extra wear and tear and neglect caused by lack of staff and problems such as the heavy bombing Swansea suffered.

The war years left their mark on Swansea, but SWT survived remarkably little affected, apart from the need to replace one body on a Leyland TD5 with an NCB utility version in 1944. There had been producer gas operation including an SWT-designed trailer used with a 1932 AEC Regent in 1940 as well as about eighteen of the later production version in 1942-44. After all the problems of operation in wartime it was a relief to see new vehicles in 1946. Unfortunately, the bodybuilding capacity at Weymann's could cope with only the first 20 AEC Regent II chassis and the second 20, built in November-December 1946, were delivered to Swansea where fitters are seen examining fourteen of them outside Ravenhill works still bearing the remains of wartime camouflage paint. Apart from a different type of vacuum brake system, they had very similar mechanical design to the 1937 batches, with 7.7-litre engine and 'crash' gearbox.

Chapter Four: The exclusively AEC years

Swansea and the surrounding area proved to be a major target for enemy air raids during much of the war period, there being some 44 such attacks between June 1940 and February 1943. Apart from the docks and various industrial installations there was the oil refinery at Llandarog, with its oil storage tanks and these are believed to have been the main target. However, the town centre was completely destroyed, and the raids were the worst in south Wales, resulting in 387 deaths and 802 premises destroyed.

Remarkably, only one bus body was destroyed, though many were damaged. Early in the war years, 28 buses were impressed for military use, including the ten 1933 AEC Regal saloons and eighteen of the petrol-engined Dennis Lancet models. Very unusually, not only did SWT receive none of the wartime utility or 'unfrozen' buses allocated to most fleets in 1942-45 but no vehicles of any kind were added to the fleet during the whole wartime period. The modern fleet of double-deckers doubtless helped to allow efficient coverage of essential services and the Mumbles Railway also played a valuable part, for passenger figures on that line reached unprecedented heights—in 1945, they totalled 4,995,000, over four times the 1938 figure. The big 106-seat cars were of particular value in carrying what would nowadays be called commuter traffic, including many peacetime motorists unable to use their cars when no petrol was available for any but priority users. A surplus of vehicles allowed some to be hired to several other operators.

On the other hand, had tram operation still been continuing in Swansea itself, it might well have been abruptly ended by the bombing, such was the damage to the centre of the town. There were many other difficulties, but they were overcome by flexibility and when necessary unorthodox methods.

Women were recruited to take over as conductresses in place of men on war service. Producer gas conversions, using the usual form of trailer-mounted plant, were used to save the imported fuel that was subject to submarine or bombing attack, though as in most fleets, normal operation was resumed as soon as permitted by an improvement in the supply situation.

The return of peace brought renewed availability of wider choice in vehicle supply. Late in 1945 AEC resumed production of chassis which in all but small details were similar to those of the 1937 tram-replacement Regent models but now designated Regent Mark II. A high proportion of these chassis received Weymann metal-framed bodywork and this combination thus conformed to South Wales standard, though the body styling was of the type with unbroken curved profile by then standard.

The first 20 post-war buses of this AEC

By chance, it happened to be South Wales' first post-war bus that was nearest the camera in this scene in Swansea. It comes from SWT's archives and the original caption reads 'Traffic congestion at High Street Station'; although the flowing line of cars would hardly rate as congestion nowadays, it doubtless did around 1950. The proportion of double-deck buses, out-numbering the cars, is also noteworthy. Number 264 (DWN 641) was the first of the 20 AEC Regent II buses with Weymann highbridge 56-seat bodywork completed in 1946. Behind

it is seen ACY 23 of the 1937 batch of Regents, by then numbered 224 and evidently newly reconditioned — it was to survive until 1957, only a year before the demise of 264. The third bus was a lowbridge Regent III, followed by one of the Metro-Cammell-bodied Albion Venturer CX19 models of United Welsh, with further SWT Weymann-bodied Regent buses. The cars, a mid 'thirties collection led by a Ford 8, Morris 8 and original-series Minor, show how scarce post-war cars still were.

Number 273 of the 1946 batch of AEC Regent II buses was quite badly damaged before entering service. The body was more quickly repaired than the chassis so it was transferred, retaining that fleet number, to one of the new chassis awaiting bodying and the resulting combination registered ECY 874 as seen here, entering service in February 1947. The damaged chassis, duly repaired, retained its registration DWN 650 and, with one of the new bodies, became 304 when re-delivered in December of that year. It is seen here at the Kingsway roundabout, heading into College Street, Swansea.

Regent II Weymann combination were completed as numbers 264-283 and all but one entered service in the period between March and August 1946. The exception was quite badly damaged and the body, after repair was transferred to a chassis from the second batch of 20 for SWT, by then built and awaiting bodying. This combination, retaining the fleet number 273 allocated to the body but with a new registration number, entered service separately in February 1947. Then the remaining nineteen new chassis, plus that of the 1946 damaged bus were bodied, entering service in the November 1947-January 1948 period. Five of these were like the 1946 buses in being highbridge 56-seat models, including that on the repaired chassis, but the remainder were 53-seat lowbridge models. The fleet numbering became rather complex, perhaps because of the replacement exercise, and some numbers were not filled.

The 1949 fleet intake could be summed up by saying that there was a switch to AEC Mark III models, for all the impressive total of some 81 vehicles were either Regal or Regent models of this series. Among them were eighteen new Townhill buses, numbered 61-78. The original versions of both Regent and Regal Mark III had 9.6-litre engines, preselective gearboxes and air-pressure brakes and although there were some doubts at that time among many company operators in particular about some or all of these features, they added up to a ready-made Townhill specification. Willowbrook got the body contract, its standard design of the period having an appearance not unlike BET Federation designs of the period. The seating capacity was 34, five fewer than earlier generations of Townhill bus.

(Below) The first post-war buses for the Townhill route, delivered in 1949, were virtually standard AEC Regal Mark III models of the 9621E type with 9.6-litre engines and preselective gearboxes, fitted with Willowbrook 34-seat bodywork. Here number 65 (FCY 346) is seen ascending the steepest part of route 12, with a gradient of 1 in 5.

The 1948 delivery of completed Weymann-bodied AEC Regent II models included fifteen of the rare lowbridge 53-seat version, of which only another five, for Midland General, were made (the highbridge Weymann body was easily the most popular of all on this chassis, accounting for nearly half the total built). It remained in service with SWT until June 1960 and then, with four others, was operated for five months by Western Welsh at Haverfordwest during the building of the oil refinery.

The Willowbrook bodywork on SWT's AEC Regal III models was basically to that bodybuilder's standard design of the period but the severely rectangular Clayton destination indicator, style of entrance and other details gave the impression of an approximation to the Federation style of the period. Number 65 is again seen on the Townhill ascent.

The 7.7-litre crash-gearbox 6821A version of the AEC REgal III looked outwardly the same as the 9.6-litre model, even though its running gear had more in common with the previous generation of AEC passenger models. Here one of the 25 smaller-engined Regals with Willowbrook bodywork of 1949, number 111 (FWN 805) overtakes the similarly-powered 277 (DWN 654), one of the 1946 Regent II models with Weymann bodywork. The photograph was taken in 1950 in Oxford Street, Swansea, before the market was rebuilt.

The same 9621E model chassis, but doubtless with a higher-geared rear axle, was used for three coaches with Windover 30-seat bodywork, with numbers in a new series beginning at 1001. These were painted in a new ivory and red livery to be used for coaches until the NBC era. The coach business, which had included touring holidays in north Wales and Scotland in the early 'thirties, was being revived and SWT began to build up a reputation for high standards.

Some 25 single-deck buses for general duties were of similar appearance to the new Townhill batch, with Willowbrook 34-seat bodywork on Regal III chassis, but the latter were of the 6821A type, retaining the 7.7-litre engine, conventional 'crash' gearbox and vacuum brakes of earlier series, with reduced noise and vibration due to the use of a flexible engine mounting as the main difference, apart from the revised appearance. Another new series beginning at 101 was used for these buses but numbers 102-106 of the series had bodywork of similar layout by Longwell Green, a small concern in Bristol.

The 30 double-deckers of 1949 were all Regent III with Weymann metal-framed bodywork, 24 highbridge 56-seat and six lowbridge 53-seat. These were on the 9612A chassis, with 9.6-litre engines but crash gearbox and vacuum brakes, and this combination was to be favoured by SWT for a further 23 similar lowbridge buses in 1950.

The 1950 batches of AEC Regent III single-deckers comprised a further nine

The AEC Regent III chassis in its 'provincial' form, together with standard four-bay Weymann body, constituted one of the truly classic bus designs of its period. The first South Wales examples entered service in 1949, number 334 (FWN 372), one of 24 with highbridge bodywork being seen here. The 1949 and 1950 batches all had the 9612A chassis, with the traditional AEC crash gearbox, almost identical to that found in SWT's first Regent buses of 1932. A fuel saving of perhaps 1mpg as compared to the version with fluid flywheel and preselective transmission was obtainable, but SWT was among operators which found that gearbox failures were apt to be experienced due to the greater torque of the 9.6-litre engine, especially when operating on hilly routes.

(Above) Five further AEC Regal III buses of the 6821A type delivered in 1949 had bodywork by Longwell Green, built to almost identical design to the Willowbrook version, though readily distinguished by the windscreen outline. They were withdrawn in 1958-59, whereas most of the Willowbrook examples lasted until 1960-61. However the former 104 (FWN 633) saw further service with Thomas Bros (Port Talbot) Ltd, to whom it was sold in November 1958, as seen here. Thomas Bros was by then also a BET subsidiary and was taken over by SWT in 1970, though this vehicle had long gone by then.

(Below) Low bridges prevented the use of normal-height buses on some of SWT's double-deck routes, notably in the Port Tennant area. The last of the 1949 batch of six lowbridge AEC Regent III models is seen in Kingsway, Swansea, after renumbering to 1120 in 1958 — originally FWN 351 had been SWT's number 313. The vehicles of this era, with chromium-plated radiator shells and minor fittings looked very smart when kept in the good condition seen here. This bus was one of the last three of the batch to remain in service, being withdrawn in 1963.

(Above) The first post-war coaches for the SWT fleet were three Windover-bodied AEC Regal III models placed in service in 1949. A fleet of fourteen more outwardly similar coaches was delivered in 1950, though the chassis were now the crash gearbox 9621A model rather than the fluid transmission 9621E of the earlier vehicles and the seating capacity was increased from 30 to 33, the latter being widely accepted as an acceptable standard for a forward-control coach of the then maximum 27ft. 6in. length. The 1950 fleet, together with one of the previous year's batch, second from the far end, is seen lined up above when new, outside Ravenhill works. The last vehicle of the batch, 1017 (GCY 444), is nearest the camera.

Unfortunately the half-cab coach was about to become obsolescent, quite apart from the constant need to appear up-to-date in the tour business. The 1950 coaches began to be sold off in 1955 and the former 1012 (GCY 439) is seen after purchase in 1959 by Landsdowne Coaches of London E11, still looking much as it had when new apart from removal of fleetnames. Another operator's new Thames Trader with Duple body, seen behind it, is typical of vehicles which made what was still an impressive coach seem outdated.

The three Continental touring coaches also purchased in 1950, although also AEC Regal III 9621A chassis with Windover bodywork, differed in being 8ft. wide, the first of this width in the fleet, having full-width cabs and more luxurious seating. The bodybuilders modified the contour of the front mudguards to suit the body profile, thereby losing a little of the character of the chassis. Number 1020 (GCY 447) is seen when new posed outside Singleton Park.

The 1950 delivery of double-deckers, again 9612A-type AEC Regent III chassis with Weymann bodywork, was entirely of lowbridge buses, there being 23 in the batch. The second vehicle, number 339 (GCY 522) is seen in its official bodybuilder's portrait. All were withdrawn in 1963.

6821A-type Willowbrook 34-seat buses and some seventeen coaches, all with Windover bodywork. All the coaches were this time on the 9621A chassis, with 9.6-litre engine and crash gearbox. Three were 8ft.-wide vehicles with full-fronted bodywork and reclining seats for 28 passengers, purchased for a new venture in Continental touring — at that date 7ft. 6in. width still applied generally. The remaining fourteen were 33-seat half-cab coaches for more general coach duties — the tour programme was proving very popular.

New vehicle deliveries in 1951-52 were all Regent III Weymann double-deckers of the newly introduced 9613A variant, taking advantage of the increase in permitted length to 27ft. and the general permission to run 8ft. wide buses without seeking route approval (needed when first allowed on buses and coaches operating in Britain from 1946, and which had tended to deter their general use). There were 23 highbridge 56-seat models in 1951 and fifteen lowbridge 53-seat buses formed the main delivery in 1952.

However, an important development which took place in March of that year was the first acquisition of another operator since the late 'thirties. The Llanelly District Traction had been an outpost of the Balfour Beatty group of companies probably best known for its

In 1951, by contrast, the entire batch, again of 23 buses was highbridge. However AEC had introduced the 9613-series version of the Regent III chassis to take advantage of the 27ft. overall length by then permissible for two-axle double-deckers and they were accordingly 9613A models. The first nine, 361-369, retained the 7ft. 6in. width applicable previously but the remainder, including 371 (GWN 83) seen here were 8ft. wide. Vehicles of this width had been permissible since 1946 but individual approval had been required for the routes on which they were to run. From 1950 this stipulation was withdrawn. The extra width is most clearly evident in the cab front panel design whilst the added length was provided behind the rear axle. The photograph was taken in St. Mary's Square, Swansea, the terminus of many inter-urban and rural services before the opening of the Quadrant bus station.

Two interior views of 1950-51 vehicles give an impression of how SWT vehicles of that era looked to the passenger. On the left, one of the Windover-bodied continental touring coaches on AEC Regal III chassis. The individually reclining seats were not quite so high-backed as usual at that time, giving better forward vision than most coaches of the day. In the double-decker, number 379 (GWN

91), one of the 1951 batch of highbridge Regent III models, the curved treatment of the bulkhead windows characteristic of post-war standard Weymann double-deckers dominates the lower deck. The general proportions and especially the ceiling contour otherwise had much in common with the pre-war version shown on page 28.

bus and trolleybus operating concerns based in Nottinghamshire. The original 1911 tram system had been replaced by trolleybuses in 1932-33.

The concern had been taken into State ownership, along with other subsidiaries of the Midland Counties Electric Supply Co when electricity undertakings were nationalised in 1948.

Unlike the transport undertakings based in the East Midlands of England, however, it was not transferred to the British Transport Commission, the body controlling most of the transport systems which had come into State ownership as a result of the Transport Act of 1947 and its aftermath. Instead the South Wales Electricity Board decided

to sell it to the BET Group, thus initiating an act of what would nowadays be called 'privatisation', destined to remain unique until the mid 'eighties.

Nine of the initial fleet of fourteen Leyland TB2 two-axle double-deckers survived into SWT ownership, still with their Leyland 56-seat bodywork, based on the style used on contemporary Titan TD2 motor buses, though with a slightly more elaborate front-end design than on most of the bus version, and with full-width cabs.

Motor bus operation had also been begun in the mid 'thirties, initially arising from the take-over of three local independent operators. New purchases were AEC Regal oil-engined single-deckers, mostly seating 35, it being more than a coincidence that a model familiar to SWT was chosen, for the Balfour Beatty companies were major AEC customers. Seven examples dating from 1936-39 were handed over to SWT, all but the first three (by Beadle) having Weymann bodywork. Two more had been added in 1947 these having Strachans bodywork and then the final six were Regal III 6821A models, again lining up well with SWT practice, but with bodywork by Bruce of Cardiff, a concern associated with East Lancashire.

There were also a dozen relatively modern trolleybuses, these being double-deckers of the wartime Karrier W type, with 56-seat bodywork by Park Royal, Roe and Brush, dating from 1945-6. By the end of 1952, the trolleybus system had been replaced by motor bus services and eleven AEC Regent III 9613A buses with Weymann 56-seat highbridge bodywork were delivered direct to SWT though ordered by the Llanelly company. The venerable Leyland trolleybuses were scrapped, but the Karrier chassis all lived on, two of the

The South Wales Transport Co Ltd holds the rare distinction of having operated trolleybuses as well as an electric railway in addition to motor buses. The trolleybus involvement was very brief, lasting only from the purchase of the Llanelly District Traction undertaking on 22nd March 1952 to the replacement by motor buses later in the year. Even so, this photograph of number 6 in the Llanelly fleet, registered TH 3009, shows SWT as the legal owner. It was one of the original batch of Leyland TB2 trolleybuses, this one having entered service early in 1933. It had altered little over the years apart from the replacement of half-drop windows by sliders and the adoption of a simplified livery. The batch had been one of Leyland's first for trolleybuses designed as such, as opposed to what were basically modified motor bus chassis.

Not all British trolleybus routes ran down busy streets, and scenes not unlike this were not uncommon on the outskirts of various towns. Ex-Llanelly number 47 (CBX 913), a Karrier W-type with Park Royal bodywork of that concern's very slightly relaxed utility style, dating from 1946, is seen at the Loughor terminus. As with all the Llanelly Karriers, the vehicle lived on, the chassis being one of ten purchased by Bradford Corporation — rebodied by East Lancs, it re-entered service in 1956 and was not withdrawn until 1969.

Training of former trolleybus drivers to handle motor buses was put in hand soon after the take-over. The former Llanelly District Traction's number 44 (CBX 910), another 1946 Karrier W with Park Royal bodywork of which the chassis was also sold to Bradford and rebodied similarly, is seen here with number 208 (ACY 7), one of the 1937 AEC Regent batch with Weymann bodywork which had been purchased to replace Swansea's trams, playing a second part in the replacement of electric traction. The Swansea Improvements and Tramways Co continued in existence until 1953 though SWT ran its operations, and ACY 7 survived until 1955.

The Llanelly undertaking also had a fleet of AEC Regal 7.7-litre single-deckers, these also passing into SWT ownership. The oldest were three dating from 1936, with Beadle 35-seat bodywork, of which number 27 (TH 7761) is seen below. A pair of 1947 Regal models, including number 20 (CTH 930) seen below right, were of mechanical specification equivalent to SWT's Regent double-deckers of the same period but had somewhat angular Strachans bodywork — the proportions, with low roof line, imply suitability for use under the low bridges in the Llanelly docks area.

Among the ex-Llanelly buses taken over in 1952 were four AEC Regal models with front-entrance Weymann bodywork dating from 1938 and having the rather attractive curvaceous styling favoured by Balfour Beatty companies at the time. Three of these were involved in experiments with buses intended to carry a higher proportion of standing passengers. The photograph reproduced, taken at the rear of the ex-LDT garage, appeared in the brochure produced for the Director's visit in April 1953 and although not identified is believed to show either 22 or 24 (ABX 901 or 902), the seating capacity having been reduced from the original 35 to 28, with space for 22 standing. Number 25 (ABX 903) is identifiable in another, interior, view but that had 29-seat capacity as rebuilt and retained its front entrance rather than having the centre entrance as shown. All the pre-war ex-Llanelly single-deckers were withdrawn in 1956.

The most modern ex-Llanelly vehicles were six AEC Regal III models of the 6821A type which had 35-seat bodywork by Bruce built to allow operation under bridges in the docks area, the lowest of which, at Trinity Road, had only 9ft. headroom. Despite this, they were quite well proportioned. Bruce was a Cardiff-based associate of East Lancashire Coachbuilders, for the most part supplying municipal operators. The Llanelly undertaking, managed at the time by the South Wales Electricity Board, had taken on a character not unlike that of a municipal one.

The 1952 deliveries of new buses were all AEC Regent III 9613A models with Weymann bodywork. The last eight had been ordered by Llanelly District Traction, though built to SWT specification, and had Weymann highbridge 56-seat bodywork to a new semi-lightweight design retaining this maker's distinctive previous standard outline. They received fleet numbers which followed after the batch to be delivered the following year, No. 419 (HWN 842) being seen on a Llanelly route. They were the last buses delivered to SWT with the old-style AEC crash gearbox in its final 'wide-tooth' D162 form, intended to be more robust than the earlier D124 type. The fifteen earlier deliveries were lowbridge buses similar to those supplied in 1951, but the first eight were remarkable in that the governors were set to give a maximum engine speed of only 1600 rpm, even slower than the 1700 rpm associated with Gardner engines of that period, though with the standard gearing they gave a reasonable top speed of about 40 mph.

The last deliveries to SWT with the traditional AEC radiator were the 1953 batch of AEC Regent III models with Weymann lowbridge 53-seat bodywork, of which number 403 (HWN899) is seen here. The chassis had the new D166 all-synchromesh gearbox and were accordingly 9613S models whilst the bodywork was a lowbridge version of the semi-lightweight design shown at the foot of the previous page. Weight was cut from 7 tons 18 cwt 3 qtr for the 1952 buses of similar outline to 7 tons 6 cwt 2 qtr despite the slightly heavier gearbox without any significant drop in standards of finish. The glazing was of the flush type using rubber mouldings and there was a touch reminiscent of the London RT in the nearside wing treatment. They were withdrawn in 1965 — by that date BET companies generally followed a 12-year life formula.

Roe bodied examples going to Maidstone Corporation complete, remaining in service until 1961, while the ten remaining chassis went to Bradford Corporation to be rebodied by East Lancashire, re-entering service in 1956. They ran for a minimum of a further ten years while three were to survive until 1971 and thus among the last to remain in service in Britain.

At the Commercial Motor Show in November 1952, an example of the AEC Regal IV model with Windover 35-seat bodywork was on display in SWT livery and entered service with another similar vehicle the following year. Two more arrived in 1954, these four being the first underfloor-engined vehicles in the fleet and having a horizontal version of the 9.6-litre engine, together with preselective transmission. The remaining 1953 deliveries were fifteen more AEC Regent III with Weymann lowbridge 53-seat bodywork, the last for the fleet with the traditional AEC radiator but differing from earlier deliveries in having synchromesh gearboxes and thus of model 9613S. Also in 1953, four 1946 AEC Regal chassis with Weymann bus bodywork were on loan from the Devon General concern, another member of the BET group, during the July-August period. Another noteworthy event that year was the winding-up of the Swansea

The first underfloor-engined models for SWT entered service in 1953, being two AEC Regal IV 9812E models with the striking, if controversial Windover body design for such chassis. The 1954 order was virtually a repeat for another two, this time on the 9822E with deeper frame, and 1023 (JWN 916) of this pair is seen here. The use of rear-entrance layout is noteworthy. All four were used on extended tours and were sold in 1961-62.

The 1954 order for buses consisted of fifteen more AEC Regent III 9613S chassis with Weymann lowbridge bodywork, but the change in their appearance from the pattern that had begun in 1946 and continued with no more than gentle evolutionary development can only be described as traumatic. The chassis had the 'new look' type of front-end sheet metalwork, offered by AEC as an option at the time. In addition, the bodywork was of the Orion design then being adopted by both Weymann and its partner in the MCW organisation, Metro-Cammell. This carried the idea of lightweight construction to greater lengths than the semi-lightweight version favoured by SWT in 1952-3. Gone was the four-bay design with its graceful curves and in its place came a much more 'basic' concept, with such features as frameless roof domes with handrail attachment carried through to the outside of the corner pillars. It is significant that this drastic approach only reduced the weight to 7 tons exactly. Eight of the vehicles had platform doors and this picture of number 427 (JWN 903) strongly suggests that in this case at least they were fitted from new.

At the 1954 Commercial Motor Show, AEC introduced a new lighter double-deck chassis, the Regent V MD3RV model, and SWT received the first production batch, placing them in service the following year. Number 443 (MCY 403) was one of the ten with a highbridge 59-seat version of the Weymann Orion body; The rear destination displays were later abandoned and panelled over from c. 1961 onwards. The AEC design of concealed radiator front-end had reinstated a recognisably AEC style of grille. All these buses, and the further ten generally similar lowbridge examples, were withdrawn in 1966 although several saw further service. This particular bus, seen at the Llanelly (Railway Station) terminus, became a mobile canteen, workshop and store for Ebbw Vale Urban District Council, passing to Blaenau Gwent District Council on its formation in 1974.

Improvements and Tramway Company, its assets being handed over to SWT.

The so-called 'new look' front of the style designed by Birmingham City Transport, arrived on the final batch of lowbridge Weymann Regent III in 1954, again on 9613S chassis but these also differed by being of 56-seat capacity, hitherto associated only with highbridge buses, and having the somewhat austere Orion type of lightweight body.

A major change on the rolling stock side came in 1955, when all the vehicles delivered were of AECs then recent 'mediumweight' range. There were ten highbridge 59-seat and ten lowbridge 56-seat Weymann-bodied Regent V models of type MD3RV, with AV470 7.75-litre engine. A further generation of

Townhill buses were outwardly standard AEC Reliance underfloor-engined single-deckers with 44-seat Park Royal bodywork, then, like the Regal IV models, being of the 30ft. length permissible on single-deck two axle buses or coaches since 1950. They were unusual at that date in having the latest version of epicyclic gearbox with so-called semi-automatic operation and air-pressure brakes and thus being of type MU2RA and revived the fleet numbers series beginning at 801 not seen since the Dennis Lancet era.

Further AEC Reliance models arrived in 1956, but these were Weymann-bodied 37-seat coaches on the synchromesh and vacuum brake MU3RV chassis, supplied in two batches, of three and five vehicles

respectively. More of the Regent V mainly with light Orion body arrived, a batch of 21 highbridge 58-seat buses in 1956 being followed by 20 more in 1957.

By coincidence, the fleet numbers allocated to AEC Regent double-deckers had just reached 501 for the first vehicle of a new variant, the 30ft.-long LD3RA version of the Regent V with Weymann 71-seat highbridge forward-entrance body. The first 26 of these, which also introduced air-pressure brakes to the double-deck fleet, arrived in 1958, together with five more Weymann-bodied Reliance coaches. A renumbering exercise carried out that year put all the lowbridge double-deckers into a series beginning at 1100 with former number 288 of the 1948 batch of Regent II buses, and running up

Having the horizontal AH 470 equivalent of the AV470 engine used in the 1955-57 batches of double-decker, the 1955 fleet of eight new buses for the Townhill route were examples of the AEC Reliance model introduced in 1953. The body design was basically the Park Royal standard 44-seat design as introduced for this chassis but the SWT examples were noteworthy in being MU2RA models with the Monocontrol epicyclic gearbox eliminating the 'clutch' pedal. The first of the batch, 801 (MCY 420) is seen here — it survived until 1973, having been renumbered no fewer than four times.

The Weymann Fanfare coach body design was one of the more successful of those produced in the mid 'fifties, being favoured by several BET companies. The SWT had two batches in 1956 and another in 1958, the vehicle shown being number 1032 (NCY 626), the last of the second 1956 batch, consisting of five vehicles. These were on the standard AEC Reliance chassis with five-speed synchromesh gearbox.

(Below) The 1957 delivery of AEC Regent V MD3RV models was noteworthy in that ten of the 20 vehicles had Willowbrook bodywork — the first departure from Weymann for double-deck bodywork since the first batch of the latter in 1934. Number 494 (OCY 677), seen when quite new, shows Willowbrook's characteristic 'eyebrow' styling effect.

(Below, right) The 1958 double-deckers reverted to the 9.6-litre engine, the vehicles being further AEC Regent V models but of the LD3RA type which had been introduced to take advantage of the 30ft. length by then permissible. The Weymann bodies were of forward-entrance type, newly coming into more general favour for double-deckers. Number 503 (RCY 345) is seen in Llanelly Town Hall Square.

The AEC-Park Royal Bridgemaster was developed with BET companies which needed low-height double-deckers very much in mind, and 60 MMD, one of the early prototypes with body structure built by Crossley, was completed to SWT requirements in 1958, although used as a demonstrator at first. It is seen (left) after acquisition by SWT, becoming 1213. Meanwhile, the Company's first production examples, to the later steel-framed design with more upright profile as built by Park Royal, had been delivered. Number 1199 (RCY 369) was the first vehicle of an initial batch of four delivered early in 1959, is seen below. A further five similar buses were supplied later in the year. The low build gave an impression of greater length than the actual 30ft. dimensions. These rear-entrance Bridgemasters remained in service until 1969-71.

to 1198, the last of the 1955 batch of Regent V models.

No sooner had the lowbridge fleet been renumbered then the type of vehicle conveyed by that name became obsolete with the fleet. The side-gangway type of double-decker had considerable drawbacks both in freedom of movement for passengers and ease of fare collection for conductors. The alternative way of getting overall height to a similarly low level, retaining the centre gangway layout on both decks by lowering the level of the lower deck floor and hence the whole of the upperworks, had attracted much interest during the 'fifties. The first such vehicle was the Bristol Lodekka, introduced in prototype form in 1950, and available only to state-owned fleets, but by 1956

there were alternatives. Notable among them was the AEC-Park Royal Bridgemaster, with independent front suspension and integral construction.

A prototype vehicle was displayed at the Commercial Motor Show that year, but the design had been revised to take advantage of the newly introduced 30ft. length limit, and this slowed development. The set of mechanical units also displayed was built into a further prototype and this was completed to SWT specification in 1958. It was registered 60 MMD and ran as an AEC demonstrator for about two years, before being added to the SWT fleet in 1960. Meanwhile, the first Bridgemasters to be supplied to the SWT fleet arrived, the first batch of four delivered in 1959 carrying the low-height fleet number series from 1199 to

1202. A further five arrived later in the year, these, like the demonstrator being 72-seat rear-entrance buses. There were also a batch of seven AEC Regent V models with forward-entrance 71-seat highbridge Weymann bodywork.

Two further AEC Regent V models, based on similar 2D3RA chassis, were single-deckers. The home market front-engined Regal single-deck model had long been out of production and underfloor-engined single-deckers were too tall to pass under some unusually low bridges, having headroom of only 9ft, in the Llanelly dock area hitherto served by two 1947 AEC Regal I buses with Strachans bodywork inherited from the Llanelly and District fleet. Accordingly, suitably low-built 37-seat bodywork was ordered for them, this work being carried out by Roe, by that

The year 1959 was almost like a re-run of the heady days of the 'thirties in terms of variety of vehicle types, even though all AEC variants. In addition to the Bridgemasters, there were two distinct varieties of Reliance and Regent. Perhaps the least glamorous were five Reliance chassis of the synchromesh 2MU3RV variety with Park Royal 45-seat bodywork of the rather utilitarian BET Federation standard of the time, number 811 (SWN 982) being seen here in company with a Regal III.

Seven AEC Regent V of the latest 30ft. 2D3RA type with the newly introduced AV590 engine were delivered, though they looked very like the previous year's delivery. Several of both the 1958 and 1959 batches were delivered unpainted, exploiting the aluminium alloy panels' natural state to give a finish which was regarded as acceptable when new, the comparison at the time being with the rather drab unrelieved crimson that had been adopted as standard for the rest of the fleet. Number 533 (SWN 996) is shown here.

The next registration number, SWN 997, was carried by a contrasting vehicle, an AEC Reliance again of the 2MU3RV type but one of four with Weymann 41-seat bodywork of a design which might be described as dual-purpose in the sense of being based on the contemporary bus body shell and having coach seats. The coach aspects were carried a good deal further, however, with distinct overtones of the Fanfare design. However, they were designed to be suitable to be downgraded to bus duties, which happened in 1963. Number 1038 is seen when taking part in the 1959 British Coach Rally at Brighton.

The Llanelly dock routes required two replacement buses and contemporary underfloor-engined chassis had much too high a frame height to allow a completed vehicle to be below the maximum height acceptable. The Regent V was the nearest approach to the old-style front-engined single-deck chassis and Roe built a suitably low type of body; its design seemed to be influenced by the thought that the chassis was of double-deck type. Number 34 (TCY 102) is shown.

late date often acting as the 'special order' department of Park Royal.

More conventional single-deckers for that period also supplied in 1959 were five AEC Reliance 45-seat buses bodied by Park Royal, together with four similar 2MU3RV chassis which received 41-seat dual-purpose bodywork by Weymann.

Further Reliance models followed in 1960, the first being a further five with 45-seat Park Royal bodywork but based on epicyclic-gearbox 2MU2RA chassis, being for the Townhill route. They were also noteworthy in having dry-sump lubrication, using a separate lubricating oil tank, a feature apt to be associated with racing cars or aeroplanes but used here to overcome oil starvation problems on the hilly route. There were also five Weymann buses and three Harrington coaches on conventional gearbox 2MU3RV chassis.

Double-deck deliveries in 1960 were again split between highbridge Regent models and low-floor Bridgemaster. This time all had forward-entrance layout, the Bridgemaster being the first such to be built. These were again of AEC-Park Royal integral construction, of course, but the Regent body contract went to Willowbrook, beginning a period of association with this combination that was to continue until the last new SWT buses on this chassis arrived in 1967, although there were also other suppliers.

However, the major historical event of 1960, so far as SWT was concerned, had occurred at the beginning of the year. The Mumbles Railway had been in decline, at first gradually and then more steeply, during the 'fifties. The numbers of passengers carried fell at the same time as operating costs rose. To some degree, this was also true of bus operation, and it is significant that Swansea Corporation chose not to exercise its right to take over the bus service operated in the county borough in 1957, after the expiry of the 21-year lease which had begun with the Act providing for conversion from trams to buses in 1936.

The railway's position was more serious and an analysis revealed that £350,000, a prodigious sum at the time, would have been needed to keep the line going. Parliamentary action led to the passing of the South Wales Transport Act, 1959, for the dissolution of the Swansea and Mumbles Railway Ltd and

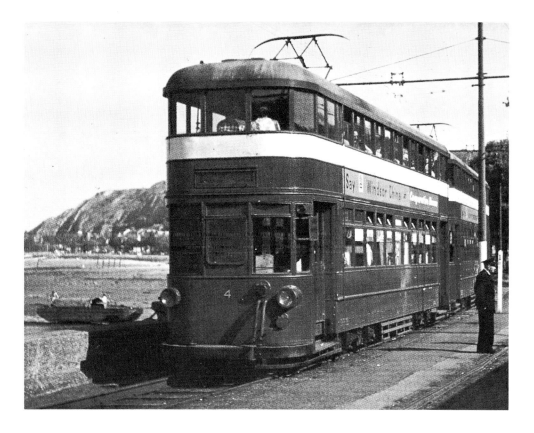

Even in its declining years, the Mumbles Railway had a unique appeal. Here a two-car train is seen leaving Oystermouth to complete its journey to the Pier along the embankment visible in the background. When it was closed in 1960, the idea of preserving railways, and working public transport items generally, was still almost unknown.

The Mumbles Railway and Pier Co and providing for the closure of the Oystermouth Railway and the Mumbles Railway.

On 5th January 1960, the railway, with its 106-seat tram-style electric railcars closed, to be replaced with a service operated by modern forward-entrance AEC Regent 71-seat double-deckers. A roadway along the approach to Mumbles Pier was equipped with an automatic barrier to prevent its use by unauthorised vehicles or pedestrians. It was the end of an era, and W. T. James, the Chairman of SWT, wrote of his feeling of sadness in the commemorative brochure issued to mark the event.

Since 1946, all of SWT's new buses had been AEC models and this continued in 1961 and 1962. Double-deckers supplied in 1961 comprised a final seven forward-entrance Bridgemasters and five further Regent V buses with Willowbrook bodywork, The single-deckers, all on Reliance chassis, comprised 22 buses for general duty and two more Townhill versions, all with 45-seat Park Royal bodywork. There were also two Harrington-bodied coaches, these having the combination of synchromesh gearbox and air brakes.

The year 1962 could be summarised as more of the same so far as Regent and Reliance models were concerned, except that the Reliance buses had

Marshall bodywork, three being for Townhill epicyclic-gearbox vehicles and three synchromesh for use elsewhere. There were two further Harrington 37-seat coaches, but the biggest intake was of Regent models, then being 24 more Willowbrook 71-seat buses.

The entire fleet had been of AEC make since the mid 'fifties, but although AEC vehicles continued to be standard for new purchases, the all-AEC era was almost at an end.

The development of a forward-entrance version of the AEC-Park Royal Bridgemaster was a logical combination of ideas found in earlier deliveries of 30ft. Regent and Bridgemaster models. The SWT once again found itself in the forefront of development for its number 1208 (WCY 888) was the prototype of this model, completed in 1960 and designated 2B3RA, as well as the first vehicle of SWT's initial batch of five. The 'utilitarian' approach to double-deck styling was just about at its height and the forward-entrance Bridgemaster had an uncompromisingly boxy appearance. Number 1208 was photographed in Castle Street on the Tycoch-Port Tennant route. This batch regularly worked on this and also the 75 and 76 services. These vehicles and the Show example, 1214, built later in the year, were all sold to Yorkshire Woollen District in 1969, surviving until 1971.

Representative of the oldest buses in the fleet of J. James and Sons Ltd, of Ammanford, shortly before the take-over by SWT in 1962 is DTH 722, a Leyland Tiger PS1, originally a single-decker dating from 1948 but one of five rebuilt on new Titan PD1 frames by the Western Welsh workshops in Ely, Cardiff for James, by then a fellow BET subsidiary, in 1954-55. Three of them, including the vehicle shown, received new bodywork built by Metro-Cammell to much the same Orion design as contemporary new SWT AEC Regent V buses. Four of these chassis had been withdrawn in 1961 but the bodies were transferred to 1950 PD2/2 chassis, in this case to FTH 680 which became SWT number 1106, running until 1963.

Chapter Five: Take-over times

On 1st September 1962, the business of J. James and Sons Ltd of Ammanford was taken over by SWT. It had been started in 1880 with horse-drawn vehicles expanding steadily and, as well as absorbing smaller concerns, was unusual among independent operators in having a co-ordination agreement with the Great Western Railway, after accidents between them. In 1950, the concern had been acquired by British Electric Traction but continued to be operated as a separate business, in line with that organisation's tendency to retain the identity of medium-sized companies. However, there had been substantial overlap of the routes operated by those of SWT and WWOC. As general costs rose and numbers of passengers began to fall, a take-over offered useful economies.

Leyland vehicles had long been favoured, largely with Leyland-built bodywork, and this policy needed no alteration to suit BET's philosophy for, although SWT's preference for AEC chassis was by no means unique within the group, Leyland was the most widely favoured make. Thus all 37 of the vehicles transferred to SWT were Leylands or, to be precise, 35 had Leyland chassis while the other two were Leyland-MCW Olympic integral single-deckers.

This renewed SWT's connection with Leyland vehicles, though this time of the post-war models, not hitherto found in the fleet. The oldest was nominally a Tiger PS1 dating from 1948, but this was the last survivor of five similar chassis rebuilt to Titan PD1 standards using new chassis frames in 1954-5 and fitted with new lowbridge bodywork by Longwell Green (as in this case) or Metro-Cammell, this latter to Orion pattern. Four of the bodies had been transferred to 1950 Leyland PD2/1 chassis.

The two Olympic 40-seat single-deckers also dated from 1950 and had been followed by three Leyland Royal Tiger PSU1/13 chassis, also of mid underfloor-engined layout, with Duple bodywork of similar capacity dating from 1951-2. A final Royal Tiger PSU1/16 of 1954 had Burlingham Seagull 39-seat coach bodywork. Later single-deckers comprised six of the lightweight Tiger

Among the most interesting of the ex-James single-deck buses were a pair of 1952 Leyland Royal Tiger PSU1/13 models with Duple 40-seat bodywork of a type built only in small numbers. One, registered HBX 50, is seen after transfer to SWT and renumbering 801. It remained in service with SWT until 1964. The PSU1-series Royal Tiger was a heavy-duty underfloor-engined model with horizontal version of the 0.600 engine used in the Titan PD2.

Leyland buses had been favoured by the James concern from the early days. This example had a body style known as the Edinburgh type from its introduction on batches of bodywork built for Edinburgh Corporation in 1920-21. The fleetname Ammanford & District was used by James in the 'twenties.

Former demonstrators have often made attractive purchases for independent operators. This vehicle, registered TF 7310, was one of the first Titan TD2 models to be built, dating from the end of 1931 and having a Leyland lowbridge body. Among its more noteworthy duties was to spend over a year as a demonstrator of the 'Gearless' torque converter transmission to Birmingham Corporation between February 1933 and May 1934, at that stage at least being recorded as one of the very few (possibly only two) TD2c models. The lack of the converter header tank and the use of a conventional Autovac alongside the bonnet suggests that a normal gearbox had been fitted by the date of this photograph showing it freshly painted, ready for sale to James, taken at Leyland early in 1935.

Two Longwell Green bodied Leyland double-deckers were among the vehicles transferred to the SWT fleet. This body had been built in 1954 on one of the Tiger PS1 chassis rebuilt to double-deck standards but in 1961 had been transferred to a 1950 Titan PD2/1 chassis, FTH 683. It is seen here shortly after the SWT take-over, with that company's name as legal owners and the fleet number altered from the original 209 to 1109. It remained in service until 1963.

Leyland bodywork had been quite a frequent choice for the James fleet but only two examples were transferred to SWT, looking very unfamiliar in this fleet despite being commonplace in many other BET subsidiaries. Number 1111 (JBX 941), seen after repainting, was a 1953 Titan PD2/12 one of the last two Leyland-bodied buses supplied to James — it survived until 1965.

It was a James vehicle, RTH 637, that had the honour of being exhibited on the Leyland stand at the 1958 Commercial Motor Show when the production PDR1/1 version of the Atlantean model was first displayed to the public. Four more completed the batch early in 1959, all having a 73-seat lowbridge version of the standard MCW body, in these cases built by Metro-Cammell. Number 230 (RTH 640) is seen here taking the corner past the Ammanford Co-op building. James' final livery, described in reference books simply as 'red' was a subtle two-tone with a slightly brownish shade set off by a single bright red band.

Cub PSUC1/1 chassis, all with Weymann 44-seat bus bodywork, two each in 1955, 1956 and 1957.

In addition to the four rebodied PD2/1 chassis of 1950, there were two Leyland-bodied PD2/12 dating from 1954 plus a single further 1957 example with Metro-Cammell Orion 59-seat body. There were also two of the 30ft.-long PD3/4 models also dating from 1957, these having similar Orion-style bodywork, built by Weymann but seating 67.

However, the thirteen most modern vehicles in the James fleet broke completely new ground for SWT, for they were all rear-engined Leyland Atlantean double-deckers. The first was particularly noteworthy as it had been exhibited on the Leyland stand at the 1958 Commercial Motor Show as one of the first Atlantean models of the production PDR1/1 type. It had the early pattern of lowbridge body designed for this model, retaining the side gangway layout at the rear of the upper deck but otherwise taking advantage of the low floor capability of the chassis ahead of the rear axle. It was built by Metro-

Cammell as were four more produced early in 1959 but the remainder, dating from later that year up to 1961, had Weymann-built bodywork of similar design.

Three further vehicles had been ordered by James but were delivered to SWT in 1963. These were Leyland Leopard single-deckers of the then new 36ft.-long type, the chassis being of the PSU3/3R type. The South Wales company had ordered the equivalent 2U3RA version of the AEC Reliance chassis with horizontal AH590 version of the AV590 engine found in the 30ft. Regent double-deckers, synchromesh gearbox and air-pressure brakes. A total of eleven were added to the fleet, and both these and the Leopard buses had Marshall 53-seat bodywork to BET Federation design. The 1963 single-deck intake was completed by six more of the special Regent V low-height buses with Roe 37-seat bodywork for service in Llanelly dock-area. replacing the six Regal III buses dating from 1950 from the Llanelly & District fleet.

The double-deck intake in 1963 was

again split between low-floor and conventional buses, but all still of AEC front-engined type. The successor to the Bridgemaster, introduced in 1962, was based on a design using a separate chassis and reviving the model name Renown, though this time used on a two-axle model. The South Wales batch had the first batch of production chassis, 3B3RA001-19, the first five of them going to Willowbrook for bodying, together with nine more Regent V 2D3RA chassis. The remaining fourteen Renown buses received bodywork by Park Royal, all these double-deckers being 71-seat forward-entrance buses.

In the event, the nineteen Renown buses were to be the only examples of the model in the fleet and subsequent new AEC double-deckers reverted entirely to the Regent V. A further 20 were purchased in 1964, 21 in 1965 and a final eighteen in 1966-67. All of these were on the synchromesh 2D3RA chassis but the 1964 batch were 71-seat 30ft. buses with the body order split between Weymann (nine), Willowbrook (six) and Park Royal

(continued on page 56)

The James fleet of Leyland Atlantean PDR1/1 models had built up to thirteen before the SWT take-over, all receiving fleet numbers adding 1000 to their original numbers. Here the last one, YTH 805, with Weymann-built 72-seat bodywork, new in 1961, by then 1239, leads a line-up of four others. They were SWT's only rear-engined double-deckers at the time and all thirteen passed to City of Oxford Motor Services in 1970.

Marshall bodywork began to figure in SWT vehicle orders in the 1962 deliveries, the company having become one of the BET group's main suppliers of single-deck bodywork. Number 1821 (TCY 665), seen in Orchard Street, Swansea, was the first of a batch of four AEC Reliance models for the Townhill routes and accordingly having the Monocontrol epicyclic gearbox. The bodywork was still of the rather plain Federation style of the time.

In 1963, the change to 36ft. overall length also brought the latest Federation single-deck design, with the style of curved windscreen later to be adopted for use in many other types of bus. Seen outside Llanelly Town Hall is the first of a batch of eight AEC Reliance models, with the AH590 engine and synchromesh gearbox, having 53-seat bodywork by Marshall incorporating illuminated advertisement panels above the offside windows. Similar bodywork was fitted to three Leyland Leopard models which had been ordered by James.

(Below) In 1962, the once-familiar AEC Renown name returned to the SWT fleet, this time applied to the newly-introduced low-floor double-deck chassis which was intended to replace the Bridgemaster. South Wales was again early on the scene in regard to a new AEC model and number 1252 (315 ECY), seen at Victoria Gardens, Neath, was one of the first batch of production chassis, being one of fourteen with Park Royal bodywork. The chassis had a front end more akin to the Regent V, with conventional front axle and leaf springs. Note the conductor, equipped with Setright ticket machine. Like most of the batch, 1252 did the usual 12-year stint of service with SWT.

The balance of the AEC Renown chassis had bodywork by Willowbrook, giving an effect not unlike a contemporary Regent with the same make of body, but having the body lowered by several inches — in effect, this was what was created. The five vehicles were on numerically the first production Renown chassis, number 1256 (536 FCY) being on 3R3RA003.

A second batch of the AEC Regent V single-deckers with Roe 37-seat bodywork was delivered in 1963, this time to replace the 1950 batch of ex-Llanelly Regal III models. Number 37 (281 DWN) is seen negotiating one of the low bridges on the routes in the Llanelly docks area involved — the lowest bridge is considerably lower, with 9ft. headroom. They were withdrawn in 1972, and sister vehicle 38 survives in preservation.

Not all SWT's routes are hilly or over narrow roads. Here a 1964 AEC Regent V, number 593 (426 HCY), one of nine with Weymann bodywork, is seen on the A48 road heading for Swansea. This batch was to a generally similar but improved version of the 1958-59 Regent V Weymann 30ft. buses. They featured the use of formica and leathercloth together with fluorescent lighting producing a more comfortable interior but the fixed windscreen by then legal made them readily distinguishable from the outside.

The body contract for the 1964 batch of 20 AEC Regent V buses was split three ways, with Park Royal building five of them to the contemporary standard which had obvious affinities to the Renown design. Number 600 (433 HCY) is seen here. Though broadly similar to the Weymann version, the wider windscreen, with slight overhang of the upper deck above it, gave quite a different look.

Willowbrook built the last six of the 1964 AEC Regent bodies, this being number 602 (435 HCY). The Willowbrook design had windows of similar depth in both decks, as well as a smoother profile, if not the subtlety of line of the pre-1953 Weymann designs. The 1964 Regents were to be the last supplied to SWT of the 30ft. length that had been favoured since 1958.

For the final batches of AEC Regent V, delivered in 1965 and 1966-67, SWT reverted to the 27ft. length, though this time continuing with the AV590 engine as used in the 30ft. versions. Willowbrook built the bodywork, the seating capacity being 64 as compared to 71 for the longer version. The first of the final eighteen, number 628 (GWN 856D), was displayed on the bodybuilder's stand at the Commercial Motor Show held at Earls Court, London in October 1966 — it had the distinction of being the last new traditional-style half-cab double-decker to be included in a national exhibition — it is seen just before being manouvered into position from the adjoining Duple stand. The last five examples to be delivered were registered early in 1967 and thus had E-suffix registrations.

(five). The 1965 and 1966-67 batches all had 64-seat Willowbrook bodies of 27ft. length. These were the last new Regent models added to the fleet and some of them were to be the last in service, when withdrawn in 1972.

Single-deck intake over this period was small, comprising three more 53-seat AEC Reliance 36ft. (11 metres) buses with Marshall bodywork in 1964 and a pair of Plaxton 44-seat coaches in 1966 and another two in 1967. All had synchromesh transmission but the 1967 coaches introduced the ZF six-speed unit.

New vehicle deliveries in 1968-69 were, by contrast, all single-deck. The 1968 batch of fifteen Reliance 11-metre buses with Willowbrook bodywork on 6U2R chassis with the AH691 11.3-litre engine were noteworthy in all having the semi-automatic Monocontrol transmission, reflecting a general change of policy on the part of major company operators. This was partly related to experience of poor clutch life on 11-metre buses, especially in hilly districts, and partly to growing interest in driver-only operation, either for immediate adoption or as a likelihood

at a later stage in vehicles' lives. Eight of the buses were intended for the Townhill services, replacing the 1955 batch of 30ft. Reliances which were modified for general use. Of the remainder, one had a wider entrance than standard, reducing its seating capacity to 52 rather than 53, as applied to both Townhill and general versions. Five vehicles had heating and ventilating equipment developed by SWT. There were also what had become the customary pair of Reliance 11-metre coaches — two more with Plaxton 44-seat bodywork and ZF synchromesh gearboxes.

The entire fleet intake for 1968 consisted of AEC Reliance 691 models, all the fifteen buses being equipped with the Monocontrol semi-automatic gearbox, the use of such transmission generally, instead of only on Townhill buses, reflecting a major change of SWT policy in line with that being adopted elsewhere. They all had Willowbrook bodywork to BET Federation design but the vehicle shown, number 1958 (NCY 289G), had a wider entrance than the rest, with double jack-knife doors. It was also one of five with a heating and ventilating system developed by SWT and having white window surrounds — one of several experiments in livery style that year.

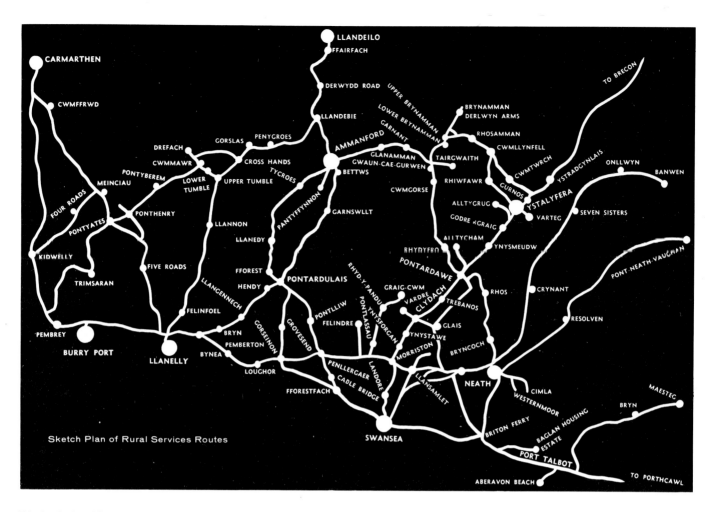

Sketch Plan of Rural Services Routes

This sketch plan of South Wales Transport's rural services dates from 1964. The pattern had 'filled-in' somewhat since the immediate post-war period, partly as a result of the take-over of James of Ammanford in 1962. However at that stage, SWT had no routes running deep into the Gower peninsular, broadly due west of Swansea, those previously operated there having been transferred to United Welsh in return for the former United Welsh routes running entirely within the then County Borough of Swansea in a deal struck in 1953. What were counted as the Swansea town services, which included those running to the south west as far as Mumbles and the Caswell Bay area, were shown on a separate plan, not reproduced here, as were the Llanelly local services.

The 1969 intake included South Wales' first examples of yet another AEC model, the Swift rear-engined single-decker, there being three vehicles with Willowbrook 48-seat bodywork with front entrance and centre exit. These were on the 2MP2R chassis version of the model, with AH505 engine, an 8.2-litre unit developed from the 'mediumweight' AH470 used in earlier Reliance models. The AH505 was also chosen for a dozen 11-metre 6MU2R Reliance models with Marshall bodywork supplied that year, all with semi-automatic transmission, though eight were 52-seat buses and four 49-seat dual-purpose vehicles. The 1969 pair of 44-seat Reliance coaches for tour duty differed from their predecessors in having Duple Northern bodywork.

Meanwhile, major events had been occurring in regard to the ownership of the company. The Labour Government of 1964-70 had adopted a policy of extending public ownership of transport undertakings. Negotiations for the purchase of the bus operating interests of BET took place in 1967 and, confronted by the threat of compulsory acquisition of at least parts of its companies, agreement was announced

The last of a long line of new AEC models to appear in the SWT fleet was the Swift, of which three examples entered service in 1969. Its rear-engined layout enabled a lower floor level to be adopted in the front portion of the body, though Willowbrook's adaptation of the Federation body design gave no external indication of the two-level seating layout within. The SWT batch had a centre-exit layout and were equipped for driver-only operation. A new series of fleet numbers was started with 701 (PWN 701H), seen here in Swansea in May 1970, but the whole numbering system was to change later that year in preparation for the merger with United Welsh, one of whose Bristol Lodekka buses is also visible. By the summer of 1971 the Swifts had been sold to London Country.

The only new vehicles delivered in 1970 were four AEC Reliance 691 coaches with ZF synchromesh gearboxes and 44-seat Plaxton bodywork of the Panorama Elite type. As received they were unregistered but numbered 1057-60 — they entered service with the numbers 176-179 in the new series and matching registration numbers were issued. Number 179 (XCY 179J) shows off the curved side-window glass which was the key feature of the Elite body style in this garage view.

by BET in November 1967. Thus South Wales Transport Co Ltd was transferred to the Transport Holding Company, an organisation formed in 1962 to hold the shares of the State-owned companies and which already included those of the Tilling and Scottish group. This was only a temporary arrangement, for under the Transport Act of 1968, the National Bus Company was set up to take over the THC interests in England and Wales and in particular those formerly in the Tilling and BET groups, coming into operation on 1st January 1969.

South Wales, unlike the majority of BET companies, did not previously have a State shareholding, due to the absence of any former railway financial interest in the company, probably because of its bad financial position in 1929-30, so it switched from private enterprise to State ownership as a subsidiary of the newly formed NBC in one go. Moreover, the complex operating pattern of company bus systems in the South Wales area was clearly open to a process of rationalisation, especially between SWT and United Welsh. The BET philosophy of allowing the continued existance of medium and larger sized companies alongside each other was out of line with Tilling policy and it was the latter that was to prove dominant in this respect.

Accordingly, control of two of the smaller ex-BET concerns, Neath and Cardiff Luxury coaches Ltd and Thomas Bros (Port Talbot) Ltd, was transferred to SWT in April 1969. In September 1970, United Welsh Services Ltd (the concern set up to take over various Red & White United Transport group subsidiaries in an area centred on Swansea) which had come into the State-owned Tilling group in 1950, was also transferred to SWT control. All three were completely absorbed on January 1971.

The background to this period of upheaval was one of decline in numbers of passengers carried coupled with ever-increasing costs. The growth of traffic congestion and staff shortages played

their part in this, tending to make services unreliable and hence playing their part in building up the vicious circle of wider use of private cars and hence starving the buses of yet more passengers while impeding their ability to provide a good service for those that remained loyal to public transport. Among the few bright spots was continued demand for SWT's high-quality tours and the 1970 new vehicle intake reflected this, consisting only of coaches, four on this occasion, reverting to Plaxton as bodybuilder for the Reliance six-speed chassis.

A significant event of 1970 was the departure of all the thirteen ex-James Leyland Atlantean double-deckers to City of Oxford Motor Services Ltd, another BET concern that had standardised on AEC buses but which found itself in need of rear-engined vehicles capable of one-man operation to help overcome a particularly severe staff shortage. In return, nine AEC Regent V models with AV470 engines and Willowbrook 63-seat bodywork dating from 1960 were taken into stock, though they were only operated for a further year.

The major merger of January 1971 brought together not only four companies with distinctive fleets but concerns with contrasting histories. Superficially, Neath and Cardiff fitted in quite happily with SWT, for its entire fleet of 26 coaches as acquired was on AEC Reliance chassis, but it was a concern with a highly individualistic character. It had been started as an independent business in 1930, initially to run a service between the two towns named but almost immediately extended to Swansea. South Wales and the other major BET company, Western Welsh, had a competitive service but N & C obtained licenses for services from Neath to both Swansea and Cardiff and through-running began again in 1932, SWT and WW having been refused.

The pre-war N & C fleet had been somewhat mixed, with Morris Commercial, Dennis and Maudslay

chassis, though Gardner oil engines had been favoured from quite early after trials with Dorman and there had been two of the rare Gloster-Gardner models. Post-war additions included AEC, Daimler, Maudslay and Tilling-Stevens coaches.

In 1953, N & C had been acquired by BET, its fleet having grown to 32, there being a half-hourly service between Swansea and Cardiff from 1954, with a large private hire business.

The unusual brown and red livery gave rise to the local knickname 'The Brown Bombers' and the individualistic nature of the concern was retained under the continuing direction of Colonel (later Sir Godfrey) Llewellyn until he retired in 1968. He was associated with many companies, including Cambrian Airways, and died quite recently. The AEC chassis tended to be favoured from the 'fifties, though a dozen of the underfloor-engined version of the Guy Arab had entered service in 1954-55. Bodywork had been purchased from various concerns, though Park Royal produced some distinctive designs, but the final fleet was split between Plaxton, Duple, Harrington and Weymann as well as the last two Park Royal examples. Neath and Cardiff was a much respected company and it was ironic that its eight-year old depot at Briton Ferry was closed a week after take-over — earlier, coaches had been garaged in Neath and at the former Swansea and Mumbles tram depot in Rutland Street, Swansea.

Thomas Bros (Port Talbot) Ltd, as a concern with that exact title, dated from 1933, when set up to take over several independent operators in Port Talbot, of which Thomas Bros had been the largest. By June 1951, when BET took over, many services were related to the needs of the local steel works. Afan Transport Ltd was closely allied to Thomas Bros, dealing with works and contract services, Davies Bros Ltd and its subsidiary, Thomas and James Ltd were also taken over though Afan Transport survived for a while as a separate

The last pair of vehicles to be placed in service by Neath and Cardiff were ordered after this concern came under SWT control, yet they retained a characteristically individualistic appearance. They were on AEC Reliance 505 chassis with semi-automatic gearbox and the Plaxton bodywork, though based on the Derwent bus outline with its resemblance to BET Federation designs, was equipped to coach standards both in the quality of seating and the provision of forced-air ventilation. The front grille was the inner part of the Panorama design. Seen here is UCY 979J, at first numbered 979 in the old SWT series but renumbered 460 in November 1970.

(Above) This remarkable line-up of Neath and Cardiff vehicles dates from about 1937. First and fifth from the right are a pair of Morris-Commercial Dictator models; the Dennis Lancet I is represented second, fourth, sixth to eighth and thirteenth; an Albion Valkyrie is third; towards the left of the line two Dennis Lancet II, two full-fronted Maudslay SF40 and possibly a Gloster-Gardner can be identified.

(Above) N & C's 'brown bombers' were often flamboyant, none more so than this Maudslay SF40 with Duple body, number 22 (ENY 68) placed in service in 1939. The SF40 — latterly given the model name Magna — was designed to allow the entrance to be ahead of the front axle, the standard four-cylinder engine being compact enough to allow entry alongside it, although a centre entrance was used here.

(Right) Two of the rare Gloster-Gardner models of about 1934 were operated, and doubtless N & C's express route allowed good use to be made of the combination of the 6LW engine and five-speed overdrive gearbox, very advanced at the time. One is seen here as running in 1950, with a Leyland metal-framed body also dating from the mid 'thirties, but of a type often sold off when its original chassis was rebodied.

(Above) Among the many interesting vehicles to have been operated by N & C was this 1938 AEC Regal, originally a Green Line coach, T460, registered ELP 184. Like many of this 10T10 type, it was sold to the United States army in 1942 but unlike most others it was not returned to London Transport after the war, passing to a Merthyr Tydfil operator, who re-registered it as HB 6138. By 1950, it was one of two such running by N & C, and is seen with original LPTB body still looking much as originally built.

(Above) The post-war AEC Regal III with fluid transmission so impressed N & C that six examples in the fleet were rebodied in 1955 by Park Royal to this 37-seat metal-framed design; HTG 442 is seen in Cardiff in April 1957. By that date, new half-cab single-deck bodywork had become very rare.

(Right) After more variety — post-war purchases included Tilling-Stevens and underfloor-engined Guy Arab coaches — in later years, N & C standardised on AEC Reliance chassis. This 1967 example, LTX 829E, had Plaxton Panorama bodywork similar to the contemporary coaches in SWT's fleet but seated 51 and was based on the lighter version of the chassis with AH505 engine, N & C favouring the six-speed constant-mesh gearbox option. It became number 164 in the SWT fleet.

(Below) The model most consistently favoured by Thomas Bros during the period of BET control was the Leyland Tiger Cub. This example of the original PSUC1/1 type was the earliest ex-Thomas vehicle, taken over by SWT when the fleets were merged. Seen here when new in 1953, it was one of a dozen with Weymann 44-seat bodywork delivered in the period up to 1958 which came into direct SWT ownership, this one receiving the fleet number 301 and remaining in service until 1972.

subsidiary. A wide variety of vehicles, many second-hand, had been operated by these firms but the older ones were discarded, resulting in a still mixed fleet of post-war coaches plus some ex-municipal double-deckers. Some ex-Devon General and Oxford AEC buses were brought in, but from 1953 a policy of standardisation on Leyland Tiger Cub single-deckers was adopted, though the AEC Reliance was also favoured at first mainly as a basis for coach bodywork. A handful of open-top double-deckers based on pre-war AEC or Bristol models was operated for a time but the fleet transferred was all single-deck.

There were 24 Tiger Cub models, ranging from one of the original 1953 batch to a final pair delivered in 1969, among the last of the model to enter service—bodywork, to typical BET pattern, was largely by Weymann but also included Marshall (responsible for the later buses), Park Royal, Metro-Cammell and Alexander. There were also three of the rare Leyland Panther Cub rear-engined model dating from

When BET took over Thomas Bros and acquired the businesses of other independent operators in Port Talbot in 1951 the resulting fleet was decidedly mixed in character. Among the vehicles taken over from Davies Bros and the closely related Thomas and James fleets was this 1949 Seddon Mark IV model, JTX 650. It remained in service until 1953.

Taken over by Thomas Bros in February 1952 was the fleet of three Bedford vehicles of Lewis & Jones of Port Talbot. Two wartime OWB models were withdrawn almost immediately but this SB with 33-seat Duple body, KTX 476, was almost new, dating from 1951, and was retained for several years. The Leyland Tiger PS1 with Whitson body also visible, HNY 377 of 1948, came from the original Thomas Bros business.

Thomas Bros had operated quite a number of second-hand double-deckers before the BET take-over, but this 1938 AEC Regent with Park Royal body, FWL 647, came from City of Oxford Motor Services Ltd in 1951 together with four others, all running until 1953.

The Leyland Panther Cub was built only in small numbers and could be described as a rear-engined equivalent to the Tiger Cub, using the 0.400 engine. Thomas Bros took three in 1966 and they were also noteworthy in having 47-seat bodywork built by Strachans, a concern then endeavouring to regain a place among the major supplier to the big operating groups. Seen here in the distinctive livery of Thomas Bros in its later years is HTG 180D which became SWT 504.

1966, using the same Leyland 0.400 engine as the later Tiger Cub, and having 47-seat bodywork by Strachans. Of the 22 AEC Reliance models, seven were coaches, the earlier examples, including three 1961-2 examples on the 2MU3RA chassis, having Harrington bodywork while the later ones were bodied by Duple. The other Reliance models comprised Marshall and Weymann-bodied 11-metre vehicles to both bus and dual-purpose specification.

The largest concern to be taken over by SWT, and certainly that with the most complex history, was United Welsh Services Ltd. By the time of transfer, the fleet had become virtually 'pure' Tilling in character, for all but four of the 154-vehicle fleet were Bristol-ECW products, the exception being four Bedford VAM70 coaches with Duple 41-seat bodywork delivered in 1969-70. There were 75 Bristol Lodekka double-deckers, ranging from LD6G models dating from 1958-9 to the final pair of FS6G dating from 1965, but also

Despite its evident regard for the Leyland Tiger Cub, extending to delivery of two of the last examples built, in 1969, Thomas Bros chose a high proportion of AEC Reliance models, with both bus and coach bodywork, through the 1960s. This 11-metre model with Duple Commander III 49-seat body was given the name 'Afan Commander' and was based on the AH505-powered version of the Reliance chassis — SWT itself took two similar-looking coaches the following year but based on the Reliance 691.

In its final years, United Welsh had favoured single-deckers and in particular the Bristol RE for most of the new vehicles placed in service. This RELL6G with ECW 54-seat body, was one of a batch of five dating from 1966, but a total of 22 basically similar RE buses were among the vehicles transferred to SWT. They had been numbered 201 upwards in the United Welsh fleet but became 601 up with SWT. Number 609 (HWN 456D) is seen in Carmarthen in June 1972 still in Tilling red but with South Wales fleetname placed on a patch of the latter's slightly darker shade.

including FLF6G, FSF6G, FSF6B, and FS6B variants. The LS6G and MW6G underfloor-engined 30ft. models graded as buses totalled 44 (some having begun life as coaches). There were 22 of the RELL6G rear-engined 11-metre buses and Bristol coaches comprised two of the SUL4A lightweight 33-seat model with underfloor four-cylinder Albion engine, three MW6G and four of the rear-engined RELH6G.

The oldest double-decker to be transferred to SWT from the United Welsh fleet was this Bristol Lodekka of the LD6G type with ECW 60-seat body, one of two dating from 1958. There were 19 Lodekka LD6G models, the remainder dating from 1959 and they were given SWT numbers in a series which followed on from the 901-908 batch allocated to the surviving ex-James Leyland PD-series buses, OCY 963 (which had been UW's 316) becoming 909. It was to survive in the fleet until 1975.

The United Welsh company had been formed with effect from January 1939 to purchase a series of former independent businesses that had been acquired by the executive directors of Red & White (later Red & White United Transport and later still United Transport) in an area centred on Swansea and thus well removed from the parent company, whose headquarters were at Chepstow. Some of the independents, who were

willing to sell to the directors rather than SWT, have already been mentioned in Chapters Two and Three. The process of acquisition and amalgamation was quite complex but brief details of the main constituents are as follows—

Gower Vanguard Motors (1920) Ltd had its headquarters in Swansea but its largest garage in Reynoldstown on the main route crossing the Gower peninsular to Rhosilly. Its origins as a motor bus operator could be traced back to 1910 when G. E. Taylor ran the first trip from Llangennith to Swansea, but horse buses had been run from 1889. By the mid 'thirties, fourteen vehicles were operated, including two Dennis Lance, two TSM, one Leyland Titan and one Thornycroft double-deckers, six Dennis saloons, one Dennis Lancet and one TSM coach, one of the TSM double-deckers and the Titan being oil-engined. The Red & White directors purchased the business in July 1936.

Bassett-Enterprise Ltd of Gorseinon had been formed in 1935 as an amalgamation of D. Bassett & Sons (Gorseinon) Ltd, purchased in July 1935 with Enterprize Motor Service (Gorseinon) Ltd, purchased in February 1934. The initial combined fleet of 17 buses was entirely of AEC make, comprising twelve Regent, two oil-engined Renown six-wheel and two 509 model double-deckers, plus eight Regal (including three oil) and two Reliance (660-type) single-deckers.

Eclipse Saloon Services Ltd, of Clydach, Swansea, purchased by the directors in January 1934, from the directors of the dealers, Arlington Motors, was running seventeen single-deckers and seven double-deckers in 1935. Leyland was the predominant make, with ten Lion and five Tiger saloons and coaches and four Titan double-deckers, plus two Tilling-Stevens double-deckers and a coach, an AEC Regent double-decker and a Thornycroft 20-seater. Two Pontardulais operators, Harris and Lewis were purchased in June 1934 by Eclipse. The Neath Omnibus Co Ltd, acquired by the directors in 1935, was merged with Eclipse in 1938.

Other concerns involved included the Blue Bird Services of T. Williams & Co of Skewen, purchased in March 1937, whereupon the fleetname became Bluebird; Windsor Services, purchased by Bluebird in November 1937 and the Gorseinon and District Bus Co Ltd, purchased by the group in November 1938.

A start was made in 1937 to include new vehicles in a common numbering scheme and adopt a standardised blue livery for the Swansea-based operators. At one time the 'Blue Fleet' was considered as a possible fleetname. United Welsh continued with the blue livery at first but after the war changed to red and white.

As these various concerns came under the executive directors' control, Albion

This scene in Christina Street, Swansea in 1932 indicates something of the strength of the presence of independent operators in the area at the time, as well as conveying the atmosphere of the period. Four of the vehicles, led by TG 1570, a 1931 AEC Regal, belonged to Bassett's of Gorseinon, the others being an ADC double-decker and two AEC Regent models with Short Bros bodywork, the latter having one of SWT's Regent buses, then quite new, between them. Bassett's merged to become Bassett-Enterprise in 1935 and was one of the larger progenitors of United Welsh.

The Gower Vanguard fleet was still largely composed of Dennis vehicles up to the early 1930s. This 1931 Dennis Lance had been built as a demonstrator to Glasgow Corporation — a fleet for whose business there was strong competition at the time — and its bodywork was to the contemporary Glasgow standard design, as generally built by Cowieson; the registration number, GG 2552, was issued by that authority. It is seen in Vanguard ownership in Swansea — note the tram track.

Enterprize was another Gorseinon operator and also favoured AEC buses. This AEC Reliance, TG 3466, was numerically the second last of the 660 series models introduced at the end of 1928 and rendered virtually obsolete a year later by the appearance of the Regal, in which the new engine first seen in the Reliance was married to the new chassis for which it was intended. In fact, Reliance sales continued in limited numbers until 1932, this Strachans-bodied vehicle dating from May of that year. The more orthodox spelling of the fleetname was adopted in the merged form Bassett-Enterprise in 1935.

Eclipse, of Clydach, Swansea, had generally favoured Leyland vehicles before coming under Red & White influence. This Leyland Tiger TS2 was photographed in March 1930 before delivery as number 12. The background indicates that the body was one of those built at Leyland's factory at Kingston on Thames.

vehicles, usually with Duple bodywork and Gardner engines, tended to be added to the fleets and this combination plus Weymann for some of the bodywork, was the favoured standard in early United Welsh days. During the war years, utility Guy Arab double-deckers and Bedford OWB single-deckers were added to the fleet. In the early post-war period Albion chassis, this time with Albion engines but again with Duple bodywork, were once more the group standard, United Welsh receiving further Albion Venturer double-deckers and Valkyrie single-deckers and coaches, but Leyland Titan, Tiger, Royal Tiger and Olympic buses were also taken into stock in some quantity and there was also a return to Guy in the 1950-52 period.

In 1950, the Red & White United Transport sold out its British bus operating interests to the British Transport Commission, then in charge of State-owned transport undertakings, and hence United Welsh, like the other bus companies concerned, came under the control of the Tilling group which managed the BTC-owned company bus fleets in England and Wales. Although

orders for vehicles that were outstanding continued to be delivered during the next two years or so, evidence of the new regime began to become evident as bodywork by the Bristol bodybuilding works or Eastern Coach Work began to appear on new or existing Albion or Guy chassis. Then, from 1952, Bristol chassis with ECW bodywork began to appear and gradually United Welsh took on the normal character of a Tilling company, complete with standard bright red and cream livery.

In 1952, United Welsh took over the Swan Motor Co (Swansea) Ltd, whose proprietors were members of the same Taylor family as the founders of Gower Vanguard. The fleet of 26 buses at that date were mainly double-deck and, over the years, Leyland, AEC and Daimler buses had been chosen. Swan had run jointly with SWT on the Swansea-Bishopston-Pennard route for many years.

Faced with the prospect of a considerably enlarged and more mixed fleet, SWT introduced a further new numbering system, put into effect a couple of months before the merger itself, in November 1970.

Its classification system indicates the new character of the fleet, the details being as follows—
91-99 double-deckers ex-City of Oxford (AEC Regent)
101-134 Coaches — small seating capacity (AEC, Bristol & Bedford)
151-179 Coaches — large seating capacity (AEC and Bristol)
201-260 Buses — small seating capacity (AEC)
301-326 Buses — small seating capacity (Leyland)
351-394 Buses — small seating capacity (Bristol)
401-461 Buses — large seating capacity (AEC)
501-506 Buses — large seating capacity (Leyland)
601-622 Buses — large seating capacity (Bristol)
701-845 Double-deckers (AEC Regent)
872-899 Double-deckers (AEC Bridgemaster and Renown)
901-908 Double-deckers (Leyland)
909-983 Double-deckers (Bristol)

The South Wales fleet had altered in character considerably but more changes were to come.

The original Blue Bird fleet had included Karrier vehicles, but when brought into the Red & White sphere of influence, the Albion-Gardner-Duple influence became evident. This Albion Valkyrie, CTX 724 was of type SPV141, with Gardner 6LW engine, and had a Duple 32-seat body. It is seen soon after entering service with the Bluebird fleetname in March 1938; similar coaches were supplied to Gower Vanguard. The fleet number 601 was an indication of the close association leading towards the complete merger under the United Welsh name. Many of the Albion vehicles of this era had long lives, this one remaining in service until 1956.

United Welsh Services Ltd was formed in January 1939 and among its first new vehicles was this Albion Venturer CX19G, one of a pair with Gardner 6LW engine and Weymann metal-framed 56-seat body, of a more modern looking style than any then in SWT's fleet and very similar to the post-war standard. It is seen in original blue livery, ready for delivery in May 1939. Number 647 (DTX 788) remained in service until 1958. Four more similar buses were delivered in the winter of 1939-40.

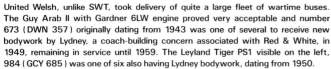

United Welsh, unlike SWT, took delivery of quite a large fleet of wartime buses. The Guy Arab II with Gardner 6LW engine proved very acceptable and number 673 (DWN 357) originally dating from 1943 was one of several to receive new bodywork by Lydney, a coach-building concern associated with Red & White, in 1949, remaining in service until 1959. The Leyland Tiger PS1 visible on the left, 984 (GCY 685) was one of six also having Lydney bodywork, dating from 1950.

The Leyland-MCW Olympic integral bus, particularly in its original 27ft. 6in.-long HR40 form, was a rare type in Britain but United Welsh received this one, 979 (GCY 680), in 1950. No further examples were taken but nine of the mechanically similar Leyland Royal Tiger were delivered in 1951-52. Albion vehicles had been favoured again in the early post-war period; the vehicle visible on the left, 910 (ECY 632), was one of nine Valkyrie CX13 with Duple bus bodywork dating from 1937.

The Swan Motor Co Ltd of Swansea sold out to United Welsh in 1952, this picture showing representative vehicles in the fleet as it stood shortly before that date. The oldest bus to be transferred was the 1937 AEC Regent with Park Royal bodywork number 15 (AWN 585), visible in the centre of the front row with another similar bus alongside. Daimler buses had been favoured for many of the post-war deliveries following wartime experience with utility examples such as the CWA6 with Duple body just visible on the left. There were eight of the Daimler CVD6 double-deck model with Daimler 8.6-litre oil engine in the transferred fleet, number 32 (FCY 732), nearest the camera, being one of four dating from 1949 with bodywork by Charles Roberts of Wakefield, which built several batches of CVD6 for various operators at that time. It was withdrawn in 1960 and the last ex-Swan vehicles followed in 1961.

The era of Bristol chassis for United Welsh following the latter's transfer to Tilling control began in a small way with pairs of KSW6G double-deckers in 1952 and 1953, but volume supply of Lodekka double-deckers and LS-type single-deckers began later that year. The oldest United Welsh vehicles to be transferred to SWT were four Bristol LS6G models with ECW 45-seat bus bodywork dating from January 1956. The use of the six-cylinder Gardner 6HLW engine in bus versions of this model was comparatively uncommon but United Welsh and Red & White favoured this combination. The offset grille was a UW peculiarity evidently resulting from a rebuild programme, and 354 (MCY 43), like many ex-UW vehicles, carried a 'Pay as you enter' sign. It ran until 1974.

Signs of the times. The problems facing NBC in general and both SWT and London County Bus Services as two of its subsidiaries with particular difficulties, led to a series of vehicle transfers. A delivery of twelve new AEC Swift 2MP2R buses with Marshall 53-seat bodywork had barely entered service with SWT in 1971 before they were sold to London Country. Here XCY 469J is seen in Llanelly bus station during its brief spell as South Wales 469, bound for Pembrey.

The same vehicle has now become London County SMW 11, and is seen in service in St. Albans. Apart from the change of livery, and the addition of sliding windows to overcome the limitations of the ventilation system, its appearance had not altered greatly, but the polished strips were removed subsequently, giving a more utilitarian look.

Chapter Six: Into the troubled 'seventies

A combination of problems, of both national and local character, made the advent of the 'seventies the beginning of a difficult period for South Wales. In many ways this applied to most members of the NBC organisation.

The balance of economics was making it difficult even for the more prosperous concerns to make ends meet and in addition, SWT was having more difficulty than most in getting applications for fares increases agreed by the Traffic Commissioners. All operators were required to justify their applications and even when there was no undue hold-up, the normal process meant that there was a serious loss of funds before the repeated increases in wages and other costs of those inflationary days could be recovered. When delay experienced, the problem could, and did, become acute.

In addition, it was difficult to recruit and retain staff. Wages in local industry were relatively high and, for the most part, the spectre of unemployment was still regarded no more than something from the dimly remembered past. On the other hand, car ownership was growing rapidly and this both helped to reduce the numbers of passengers carried and increased the congestion on local roads, helping to make the bus services unreliable and itself encouraging the drift from public transport.

Although the merger of SWT, United Welsh, Thomas Bros and Neath & Cardiff enabled economies to be made, the new larger SWT was by no means an affluent giant. It was also affected by problems elsewhere within NBC, for the former country services and Green Line sections of London Transport had been transferred to a new NBC subsidiary, London Country Bus Services Ltd, as a result of legislation. The LCBS fleet was in urgent need of vehicles suitable for one-man operation as a means of curtailing its high operating costs and it was agreed that two batches of AEC Swift buses which were to have been SWT's new vehicle intake of 1971 would go to LCBS. The first batch of twelve buses with Marshall bodywork had actually been taken into SWT stock

before almost immediately being sent off to LCBS between June and October of that year. A further 21 vehicles with Alexander bodywork were diverted before delivery. The three 1969 AEC Swift buses with Willowbrook two-doorway bodywork were also sold to London Country.

As a result, the 1971 new vehicle intake was, in effect, cut to those vehicles which had been ordered by United Welsh—five Bristol RE models with ECW bodywork—and Thomas Bros—three AEC Reliance with Willowbrook 45-seat bodywork. The Bristol vehicles comprised two RELH models with dual-purpose 49-seat bodies and three RELL 53-seat buses. To cover the gap, fourteen Leyland single-deckers, most of them fifteen years old and hence overdue for replacement on the basis of standard BET practice, were hired from Western Welsh. Half of them were Tiger Cub models and half the closely-related Olympian model, not to be confused with the double-deck of that name but integral single-deckers with Weymann

The immediate, if temporary, replacements for the almost new AEC Swift buses lost to London Country were some elderly Leyland single-deckers from the Western Welsh fleet. Number 332 (MUH 171) was one of seven purchased — it was a Tiger Cub with Weymann body dating from 1957 and typical of WW buses of its period — the integral Olympian model, of which five were included in the purchase, was outwardly very similar.

(Below) The idea of converting former coaches of the mid-1950s Bristol-ECW standard type for bus work had been pioneered by the Thames Valley company in 1964, but SWT adopted the principle to augment its fleet, beginning in 1971 with seventeen former Royal Blue MW6G models rebuilt as 45-seat buses. Number 264 (XUO 711), new in 1958 and originally owned by Western National (in those days sharing operation of the Royal Blue services with Southern National) is seen in Swansea soon after conversion in June 1972.

Noteworthy among the minority of new vehicles from the 1971 deliveries SWT was able to keep were a pair of Bristol RELH6G models from United Welsh. They were painted in a style which could be counted as a precursor of the standardised NBC dual-purpose style adopted the following year. Number 623 (XWN 623J) is seen in Cardiff on the former Neath & Cardiff concern's route — it is something of a tribute to the latter that the board in the windscreen still read 'N & C Cardiff-Swansea'.

The permanent replacements for the AEC Swift buses sent to London Country were fifteen virtually new Bristol RELL6L models with Marshall 51-seat bodywork out of a batch of 20 supplied to Western Welsh in 1971, though not placed in service by that company before transfer. The balance of five were transferred to SWT with the Neath Abbey depot in January 1972. Number 629 is seen at Neath Victoria Gardens.

body shells outwardly almost identical to the bodywork by that builder on most of WW's Tiger Cub models. Seven, including five Olympians, were purchased and ran until 1972.

The hired Western Welsh buses were intended as a stop-gap until fifteen Bristol RE buses that had been ordered by, and were delivered to, that company could be transferred to SWT to replace the Swift buses taken from the SWT fleet for LCBS. These differed from the RE models which had come into the fleet via United Welsh sources, being RELL6L models with Leyland engines and having 51-seat Marshall bodywork of BET style.

There also began an intake of second-hand vehicles from other NBC subsidiaries. Such transfers were by no means uncommon within NBC fleets, and reflected the existence of surplus vehicles in many companies as services were cut back while others had operational needs, often of a short-term nature until service patterns could be

rationalised. In SWT's case, many were Bristol MW6G models which had begun life as 39-seat coaches but were converted to 45-seat form with bus seats, destination boxes and power-operated doors before entry into service. The first seventeen were from the Royal Blue fleet, dating from 1958 and some were converted by Western National, operator of the Royal Blue services, and others by Western Welsh or in South Wales' own workshop at Ravenhill before entering services. Midland General also contributed three Bristol Lodekka double-deckers, of similar age, one being of the rare 30ft. LDL6G type.

In 1972, the new vehicle intake was again modest — five more AEC Reliance models with Marshall dual-purpose 49-seat bodywork and three more Bristol RELL6G buses with ECW 53-seat bodywork, the last again emanating from a United Welsh order. There were fifteen more conversions of Bristol MW6G or similar coaches, the two oldest actually being of the

outwardly similar but semi-integral LS6G type, the vehicles comprising five each from the Royal Blue, Oxford (originally South Midland) and United, these last-mentioned, dating from 1961, being somewhat newer than the others. There were also eleven 1957 MW6G models which had always been buses, from the Red & White fleet.

More significant in numbers and in wider implications were two transfers of depots with services, staff and vehicles from Western Welsh. The name Western Welsh had originally related to the association with the Great Western

Among the more interesting buses transferred with the Neath Abbey depot from Western Welsh in 1972 were four AEC Renown double-deckers dating from 1965 and with chassis generally similar to those of SWT's own batch of 1963, but with 67-seat bodywork by Northern Counties, number 877 (BKG 718C) being shown.

At Haverfordwest, the double-deck allocation consisted of four 1969 Leyland Atlantean buses, also with Northern Counties bodywork, in this case seating 73. They were based on the PDR1/3 chassis with drop-centre rear axle allowing low overall height with conventional gangway layout. Number 903 (PKG 375H) is seen above.

Railway and the company's most important operating area had always been centred on Cardiff, covering a sizeable part of south east Wales. Even so, the name had some geographical justification in terms of nominal territory even if much of it was thin in density of traffic. Therein lay the problem which arose when operators turned to local authorities for financial support to keep loss-making services running, for Western Welsh routes received very little. Severe cut-backs of the network, including depot closures, resulted and eventually it was decided to transfer all Western Welsh operations west of Porthcawl to SWT, nominally to have effect from 1st January 1972. Expressed thus, this implied a large increase in SWT's territory at the expense of that of WW, which now extended only about 25 miles westwards of Cardiff, barely extending beyond SWT's home territory.

In practice, the original scheme was modified and only Western Welsh's Neath Abbey depot operations were transferred to SWT on 1st January 1972, being followed by Haverfordwest depot and its activities on 27th March. Western Welsh's depots at Newcastle Emlyn and

New Quay were transferred to Crosville, it being considered that they stood a better chance of benefitting from the deals for support that company had negotiated in the Cardigan area.

The Neath Abbey transfer brought in 35 vehicles, and that at Haverfordwest some 22, basically the depots' operational fleets except that some internal transfers had been made within Western Welsh to bring the range of types involved more into line with the South Wales fleet. This applied more particularly to Neath Abbey, where the buses transferred included the remaining five of the 1971 batch of Bristol RELL6L with Marshall 51-seat bodies and four AEC Renown low-floor double-deckers with Northern Counties 67-seat bodywork dating from 1965, all of which had been switched to Neath Abbey in place of Leyland buses kept by WW. The remainder of the Neath Abbey fleet comprised nineteen AEC Reliance and seven Leyland Tiger Cub models largely with 41-seat dual-purpose bodywork by Marshall and dating from 1966-67 although including some older examples by Willowbrook or Park Royal of 1959-65 and a minority of 43-seat bus versions.

The Haverfordwest transfer was all-Leyland, except for one 1965 AEC Reliance 51-seat coach with Duple Northern body which had begun life with Neath and Cardiff and had already been in the SWT fleet until going to WW in 1971 but now transferred back by special arrangement. This time the four Leyland Atlantean double-deckers, 1969 PDR1/3 models with Northern Counties 73-seat bodywork, were included among the buses handed over to SWT, unlike those of this type at Neath Abbey, thus reintroducing the type to the fleet after the sale of the ex-James examples in 1970. They were given numbers 901-904, originally allocated to some of the ex-James buses in the 1970 renumbering, but never carried.

Of the single-deckers, fifteen were Tiger Cub models and the remaining two Leopards, with bus or dual-purpose bodywork by Park Royal, Metro-Cammell, Marshall, Willowbrook or Weymann and dating from 1959-65 in the main, apart from one vehicle new in 1957 and one in 1969.

After the complexities of the previous few years, 1973 brought a return of standardisation in the intake of new

buses, albeit on a fresh basis, as SWT received its first intake of Leyland National buses, numbered 701 upwards in a series previously used by AEC Regent double-deckers, but now gradually being vacated as they were withdrawn. Production of this integral-construction model, soon to be as familiar throughout the country as NBC's single-deck standard model had begun the previous year and the Company's first allocation comprised 28 examples of the 11.3-metre version with single-doorway 52-seat bodywork. The poppy red NBC bus livery had been adopted from the previous August, with white for coaches and the combination of the two for dual-purpose vehicles.

Additions to the coach fleet in 1973 took a rather less predictable turn, with a chassis make not previously purchased for new vehicles by SWT. This was Bedford, though there was a sense of continuity from the four VAM examples taken over from United Welsh. There were twelve in the 1973 order, all with

The first Leyland National buses for SWT arrived in 1973, all 28 being of the 11.3-metre 52-seat single-door type which was to remain the company's usual standard for this type. This original model with 510 engine of 8.2-litre capacity was to continue being delivered to SWT until 1979. Number 726 (NWN 726M) is seen at Abbey Works, Margam — the steel industry had long been an important source of employment and hence special services to the works here and at Port Talbot were justified.

As the new order arrived, so the old faded. The last new AEC vehicles for South Wales with bodywork of bus outline had been delivered in November 1971 but did not enter service until the following year. Number 466 (BWN 466K) was the last of five examples of the 6MU2R chassis with AH505 engine, semi-automatic transmission and Marshall 49-seat dual-purpose bodywork and is seen in Llanelli in June 1972 soon after entering service.

The 1973-74 period introduced both Bedford and Ford lightweight models to the SWT fleet, a complete departure from the company's previous practice extending back to the beginning, unless one counts emergency purchases associated with World War I. All were bodied by Willowbrook, the Bedford models being chosen for coaches using this bodybuilder's recently introduced Expressway design – number 220 (PWN 220M), seen at the top of the page in Neath Station Square, being one of nine on the shorter YRQ chassis with 45-seat bodywork. The 35 buses on Ford R1014 chassis, had bodywork of Willowbrook's design as introduced in the late 1960s and combining the BET windscreen with a grille reminiscent of Duple coaches – Willowbrook had been a Duple subsidiary, though independent since 1971. Number 230 (PWN 230M) is seen running into Swansea on the service from Llanelli.

Willowbrook bodywork but nine being YRQ models seating 45 while three were one of the 11-metre YRT version with 51-seat bodywork, of which the last two entered service early in 1974. Both YRQ and YRT models had underfloor engines.

Further lightweight models were some 35 Ford R1014 buses with Willowbrook 45-seat bodywork, delivered in 1974. This 10-metre chassis had a similar layout to the Bedford VAM, with engine and entrance ahead of the front axle. Later in the year, a further 25 Leyland National 11.3-metre buses were placed in service, the first eight having

50-seat capacity but the rest being 52-seat versions.

The 1974 deliveries were completed by three vehicles which could be counted as maintaining much older South Wales traditions, in the form of AEC Reliance coaches of the 6U3ZR type with ZF six-speed synchromesh gearboxes and Duple 49-seat bodywork. There had been new AEC vehicles for SWT's tours fleet for half a century. This long association with AEC was soon to come to an end, however, as the last vehicles of this make were delivered in 1975.

These were again Reliance-Duple 49-

seat coaches, but this time on the 6U2R chassis with semi-automatic Monocontrol transmission and were painted in the dual-purpose poppy red and white livery, so could be counted as more in the Neath & Cardiff tradition. Even so, their arrival signified the end of a remarkably durable association between this manufacturer and customer though AEC vehicles continued to serve the fleet in inevitably diminishing numbers for another decade. However, a second-hand Marshall-bodied AEC Reliance from the Oxford fleet was taken into stock.

Also arriving in the earlier part of 1975 was another Bedford YRT with Willowbrook 51-seat coach bodywork, replacing a vehicle which had been a fire casualty, but another vehicle which could be included as part of SWT's leisure service fleet was an open-top double-decker. This originally dated from 1953, being a Bristol KSW5G with ECW body, of lowbridge type as built but converted by the removal of the roof. It was purchased by SWT in damaged condition in September 1974 but repaired using parts from an ex-United Welsh breakdown vehicle of basically similar KSW6G type. It entered service in poppy red livery in May 1975 on service 1, running from Swansea to Limeslade, past Mumbles Head and thus in the long tradition of pleasure travel in that direction. However, it is also worth remembering that Thomas Bros had run open-top double-deckers in the 'sixties, beginning with ex-Brighton Hove & District Bristol models but also including two AEC Regent buses from Devon General and Eastbourne Corporation respectively.

To a large extent, SWT fell into line with general NBC vehicle policy from the mid 'seventies. The main intake in 1975-76 comprised 33 more 52-seat Leyland National buses, the later examples being of the mildly revised Phase 2 type. That year's coaches marked a switch to the Leyland Leopard, for five PSU3C/4R examples with Duple Dominant Express 49-seat bodywork painted in dual-purpose livery were added to the fleet. Towards the end of the year, seventeen more Ford R1014 models arrived, this time with Duple Dominant 43-seat bus bodies, one being displayed at the Commercial Motor Show at Earls Court, London.

The local government changes of April 1974 had created a different pattern of county boundaries and, in the years that followed, some changes in policy. The former Carmarthen, Cardigan and Pembroke were combined to form Dyfed, while the big and populous area of Glamorgan was split into three new counties, South, Mid and West. The more sparsely populated Dyfed continued to be a problem area and severe cuts in services in the Ammanford areas in January 1977 reduced the number of buses in the local depot from 27 to seven.

The last of a long line of new AEC vehicles for South Wales Transport arrived in 1975 in the form of five Reliance coaches with Duple Dominant 49-seat bodywork. They were officially classed as dual-purpose vehicles with slightly less luxurious interiors than the final three Reliance touring coaches which had been delivered the previous year, which had 44 or 49-seat capacity in basically the same body shell and accordingly were painted in the all-white National coach livery. The 1975 vehicles had semi-automatic transmission, then coming into general favour on NBC group coaches. The poppy red and white NBC corporate image livery suited the Dominant body style quite well and gave an effect quite close to SWT's own final livery for such vehicles. Number 469 (HCY 469N) carries a London service sticker in this view.

(Left) South Wales Transport had not operated any open-top double-deckers since the withdrawal of the AEC S-type buses of the 1920s and had also never previously carried fare-paying passengers in any of the Bristol K-type buses of the pre-Lodekka era, the four in the United Welsh fleet having been withdrawn before the amalgamation. However, WNO 484, an ex-Eastern National 1953 Bristol KSW5G with ECW body converted to open-top was restored to smart condition, at first in standard poppy red, numbered 500 and placed in service on a new service to Limeslade in May 1975, this picture showing it on one of the first runs.

The Bristol VRT rear-engined double-decker, by then well established in most NBC fleets, made its first appearance in that of SWT where twelve entered service in the early part of 1977. They had ECW 74-seat bodywork to the familiar low-height design, taking advantage of the model's capability to allow centre-gangway layout on both decks within the 13ft. 8in. overall height but were noteworthy in having Leyland 501 engines rather than the more usual Gardner 6LX series. These were basically similar to the unit used in the Leyland National, though in vertical form, and it was doubtless reasoned that there would be benefits from using similar engines in SWT's standard single- and double-deck types. The fleet numbers began at 905, following on from the ex Western Welsh Atlanteans, and thus this series gradually became one for rear-engined double-deckers. A further sixteen

The Leyland National single-decker soon became familiar on SWT routes, including the Townhill services so long the preserve of specialised buses — more power had rendered them less of a problem. Here number 761 (JTH 761P) of 1975 is seen on the 13 Townhill Circular.

A further batch of Ford R1014 buses was delivered in 1976 but on this occasion the seventeen vehicles involved had 43-seat bodywork by Duple, to the Dominant bus design introduced a couple of years previously. Number 272 (NCY 272R) is seen above in its official bodybuilder's portrait. Outwardly similar number 275 of this batch was of interest in having an Allison automatic gearbox.

generally similar buses began delivery later in the year, though the last three were convertible open-toppers, and there were also ten more National 52-seat buses and another pair of Duple Dominant Express Leopards, this time of PSU3E/4R type.

However, a complete departure from previous practice was the appearance of SWT's first minibuses. Two Ford Transit

16-seat buses having the Strachans version of the standard 'bread van' body had been acquired from the Oxford fleet, when they had been used for a dial-a-ride experiment in the Abingdon area in 1972. Christened 'The Gower Pony', they were used on a service linking Gower and Mumbles via four bays in a beautiful but sparsely inhabited area.

South Wales Transport was later than most NBC subsidiaries in receiving its first examples of the Bristol VRT double-decker with ECW body, which had become a familiar sight in most small fleets by the early 1970s. In fact, no new double-deckers had been purchased since the last AEC Regent buses for the fleet in 1967. Ten years had passed by the time the first dozen VRT models entered service in 1977. They were of the VRTSL3-501 type — in other words series 3 buses with the Leyland 501 engine, and SWT was to be unusual in standardising on this power unit instead of the more popular Gardner for all the new examples of this model purchased. Number 911 (OCY 911R) of the first batch is seen in Swansea.

Many of the numerous transfers of vehicles between NBC subsidiary companies which took place in the mid 1970s involved vehicles that had been in service for some time, but the then Leyland Leopard coaches transferred from Midland Red early in 1976 had not even entered service. Something of that indefinable sparkle of a brand new vehicle is evident in this garage view of number 185 (JOX 443P). They were on PSU3C/4R chassis with the Leyland 680 engine and the Pneumocyclic five-speed gearbox — the PSU3C series chassis had been introduced in 1974 and incorporated various brake system modifications including the introduction of the spring parking brake. The Plaxton bodywork seated 47 and was of the Panorama Supreme type.

The first Leyland Leopard vehicles to be initially ordered by SWT were five further PSU3C/4R chassis but with Duple Dominant 49-seat bodywork painted in the dual-purpose livery, the first of the batch, 472 (NCY 472R) was photographed at Haverfordwest depot with the blind set for the Haverfordwest — Carmarthen service. With no chassis maker's emblem on display, these vehicles were externally all but indistiguishable from their AEC Reliance-based immediate predecessor — compare with the photograph on page 71.

The minibus first appeared with SWT in 1977, when two vehicles that had been operated previously by City of Oxford Motor Services Ltd were acquired for use on the 'Gower Pony' service. Number 98 (NWL 704M) had been new to that company in 1973, being one of a number of vehicles used for experimental services. The Ford Transit in the diesel-engined version of its original form with slightly protruding bonnet was used as the basis of the standard 16-seat conversion of the parcel-van body, at that date carried out by Strachans. It is seen posed against a background of Swansea Bay, with Mumbles Head and Pier visible in the distance, the area where it was to operate.

The use of the Welsh form of the fleetname, De Cymru, on the offside of SWT vehicles began in the winter of 1977-78. Among the first vehicles to receive it from new were the batch of fourteen Bristol VRT double-deckers of which numbers 931 and 926 (RTH 931 and 926S) are seen here in the yard at Ravenhill works. Number 931 was one of a pair of vehicles with detachable top covers to allow summertime operation as open-toppers — note the double upper-deck waist moulding. Visible in the background is CCY 994C, one of the 1965 batch of AEC Regent Vs with Willowbrook bodywork which had been renumbered for a second time the previous May as 874 and was about to be withdrawn.

Increased consciousness of the value of preserving the Welsh language led to a decision to show the fleetname in its Welsh form, De Cymru, on the driver's (right-hand) side of the vehicle and this began to appear during the winter of 1977-78.

From a new vehicle viewpoint, the rest of the 'seventies, and indeed into the early 'eighties, largely followed a standardised pattern. Leyland National deliveries continued steadily, the single-door 11.3-metre 52-seat version remaining the sole choice, until the total delivered reached 115 with the arrival of number 815 at the end of 1979. Similarly the Bristol VRTSL3-501 with 74-seat body remained SWT's standard, the sequence running uninterrupted until

91 had arrived towards the end of 1980, fleet numbers running up to 995.

The PSU3-series 11-metre Leyland Leopard continued to be chosen as the basis for coach bodywork, another pair with Duple Dominant Express 49-seat bodywork being delivered in 1979. The 1980 batch of three had Willowbrook 003 Express bodywork and were noteworthy in being delivered in white but receiving broad red bands before entry into service. At the end of 1980 it was announced that ten more Willowbrook-bodied Leopards were on order but it was not until the following winter that eight of these appeared, beginning a fresh fleet number series at 101. These were further 003 Express 49-seat models and this time were in the

Express West livery used for joint SWT, National Welsh and Bristol Omnibus services linking Bristol, Cardiff and Swansea and Llanelli, Carmarthen or Haverfordwest. This had been introduced with existing vehicles the previous September. Two more basically similar models had 003 bodies with 46-seat bodywork.

As with other NBC fleets, there was a decline of interest in lighter vehicles, for a time at least. The Gower Pony service had proved quite successful, but at that stage no further minibuses were required, so the only purchases were two Bedford CF models with the angular but more stylish Reebur 17-seat body which replaced the pair of Ford Transit buses early in 1980. No larger

This Leyland Leopard PSU3E/4RT with Willowbrook 003 Express 51-seat bodywork was one of a batch delivered in white livery but which received the red band shown before entering service in the earlier part of 1980. Number 173, new as 481 (BTH 481V), is seen here. The index marks TH and EP, previously issued by Carmarthen and Montgomery county councils respectively, had been issued by Swansea local vehicle licensing office since the reallocation of marks associated with the reorganisation of local government in 1974. Accordingly, they had subsequently appeared on SWT buses along with the long-familiar CY and WN combinations.

The new Quadrant Centre in Swansea put a shopping centre directly alongside a central bus station facility. The numbered bays provide for head-on loading from the enclosed waiting area for passengers. Here Bristol VRT number 907 (OCY 907R) is seen departing for Llanelli.

By the time the Quadrant Centre came into operation in 1979, the SWT single-deck fleet had become standardised on the Leyland National as the principal full-sized single-decker. Seen here is number 815 (AWN 815V) the last of 115 examples of the version with Leyland 510 engines that had been placed in service between 1973 and 1980. This view also shows the Debenhams department store adjoining the bus station.

lightweight buses were added to the fleet for about four years after the 1976 order for Ford R1014 models had been fulfilled.

Meanwhile there had been other developments, as well as the first signs of a major change in economics and operating climate. On a local level, the building of a new bus station as part of a city centre reconstruction in Swansea put in hand in 1978 resulted in the Quadrant Centre development, with covered accommodation for bus and coach users adjacent to a modern shopping area.

An organisational change which had taken place in September 1977 was the regrouping of NBC's structure to produce a region entitled Wales and the Marches, in which all the Welsh subsidiaries, plus Crosville with its immense coverage of the northern part of the principality, were included. In a more immediate sense, SWT did not appear to be greatly affected by this, save perhaps in the use of the De Cymru version of the fleetname, but the increased contact with the Welsh Office was eventually to influence such aspects as better communications between north and south.

The Gower Pony service received new rolling stock in 1980, when the original Ford Transit buses were replaced by a pair of Bedford CF chassis with the angular Reeve Burgess 17-seat body. Here number 97 (CEP 197V) carries the Gower Pony emblem which had also been fitted to the Transit models.

Chapter Seven: The competitive 'eighties

South Wales was not unused to declining industry. Coal mines eventually became worked out and even in times of prosperity, a proportion of them closed. However, the recession of the early 'eighties was a different order and both coal and steel industries, so long a key part of the local economy, were hit.

The return of the Conservative Government in 1979 and the Transport Act of 1980 put renewed emphasis on competition and at first this was largely concentrated on coach services. However, there was more use of a marketing approach for bus services, too, with the Port Talbot local services

given an 'Afanway' identity from June 1980 which those in the Haverfordwest area became 'Cleddau'. Various forms of local unlimited travel ticket were introduced with names such as City Rider, Llanelli Town Rider, Master Rider and Master Rider Plus, the last covering all SWT and National Welsh bus services. A sign of the times was the Jobseeker ticket introduced in 1981, available to registered unemployed people which allowed bus travel for a maximum return fare of 50p, originally.

The intake of new buses tended to slow down. The Leyland National 2, with Leyland 680 engine instead of the 500-series and length increased slightly

to 11.6 metres, appeared in production during 1980 and SWT was among early recipients with five examples numbered 816-20 but they were to be almost the last of the species delivered new to the fleet, only one more, number 829, being purchased in 1981. Instead, eight second-hand M-registered examples from the East Kent and eight L-registered models from London Country were taken into stock, two of the latter taking up numbers 718 and 776 left vacant by fire casualties. There were also two second-hand Bristol RE purchased from Bristol Omnibus Co.

However, there was a relatively sizeable order for lightweight buses

The idea of using names with a local identity for bus services was widely adopted by NBC in the 1979-81 period, linked to the reorganisation of services which resulted from the Market Analysis Project surveys. 'Afanway' was related to the Afan river running through the Port Talbot area and is seen on one of the Leyland National buses purchased from London County Bus Services in 1981. Number 831 (NPD 144L) had been one of a batch originally supplied for use on Green Line services, the seating capacity being 49. It is seen in company with a dual-purpose Bristol RE with ECW body.

Further lightweight vehicles using Duple Dominant bus-style bodywork were delivered in 1980-81 but this time on Bedford YMQ chassis with Allison automatic transmission rather than the Ford R-series examples of 1976. There were eleven with 43-seat bus bodywork, number 287 (FCY 287W) being seen when quite new.

The seven basically similar Bedford YMQ — Duple vehicles had high-backed seating and were accordingly in the standard NBC dual-purpose livery with white upperworks, although the seating capacity was 45. Number 280 (FCY 280W) is seen here.

Operation of AEC Regent buses by SWT, and also by the whole NBC group, ended in February 1982. The last few vehicles had been kept in service because of the awkward Plough Corner on the Swansea-Pennard route which the 27ft. version of the Regent could negotiate, unlike longer buses in the fleet. Number 889 (GWN 867E) is seen near the end of its days at the Swansea terminus — it was to be the last of all in service, on a town route, on 27th February 1982.

To replace the Regents on route 14, five of the special short-chassis Bedford YMQS model were purchased, these having Lex Maxata 37-seat bodywork. Number 298 (LCY 298X) is seen at the Quadrant Centre soon after entering service early in 1982.

delivered in the winter of 1980-81, this time for eighteen Bedford YMQ chassis with Duple Dominant bodywork, seven finished in dual-purpose manner and the remainder as buses, seating being for 45 and 43 respectively.

However, more unusual was an order for five of the shortened version of the same Bedford chassis, the YMQS. These received Lex Maxeta 37-seat bus bodywork and were intended to meet a requirement for vehicle capable of negotiating a tight corner on service 14 from Swansea to Pennard hitherto operated by 27ft-long AEC Regent V buses. These latter were the final survivors of SWT's once massive Regent fleet, retained because of their ability to negotiate the corner without reversing.

The Bedford-Lex vehicles replaced the Regents on route 14 on 2nd February 1982, but the latter continued to run until final journeys on traditional Swansea city routes were run on the 27th of that month by number 869 (GWD 867 E), one of the final batch of 2D3RA type buses with Willowbrook 64-seat bodywork dating from 1967 — the other final survivors were similar buses from the 1965 and 1966 batches. This was also the last AEC Regent operation within NBC. There had been Regent buses in SWT's fleet since 1932 and this period of almost half a century had seen the peak of the Company's growth as well as harder times.

The look of the fleet was changing rapidly. The last remnants of the pre-

1971 merged fleets were disappearing and indeed the last Thomas Bros and Neath & Cardiff vehicles had gone the previous autumn. The last AEC Reliance bus, number 466 dating from 1972, was to follow later in 1982.

Meanwhile, the coach side of the business was reflecting the opportunities for expansion that had been opened.

An important development was the decision to transfer the activities of National Travel (South West) in Swansea to SWT, with effect from April 1981. This was sufficient to tip the scales against a threatened closure of Brunswick depot as the coaches transferred from National Travel were moved from that concern's North Dock depot to Brunswick. The 23 coaches, all

Oldest of the coaches transferred from National Travel (South West) in April 1981 was YDF 327K, a Leyland Leopard PSU3B/4R with Plaxton Panorama Elite II 47-seat bodywork that was originally delivered to the Black and White Motorways fleet based at Cheltenham in 1971, numbered 327. It is seen here at the Quadrant Centre after becoming SWT 186.

Following its formation National Travel (South West) had continued to use as headquarters the former Black & White base in Cheltenham, so its vehicles also often had the traditional Gloucester registration marks. Seen here as SWT's 195, this Leyland Leopard PSU5C/4R had been one of a batch with Duple 50-seat bodywork placed in service towards the end of 1979, then numbered 281 and registered GDF 281V accordingly.

The 12-metre PSU5-series of Leyland Leopard was becoming more widely used within NBC subsidiaries by 1980, and KAD 349V, seen here in Cardiff when still bearing the 'South West' fleetname of National Travel (South West), was one of four PSU5C/4R chassis with Plaxton Supreme IV 57-seat bodywork delivered in the spring of 1980 and transferred to SWT the following April, this one becoming number 156. The National Express fleetname was introduced at the end of 1980.

The ExpressWest limited-stop service linking Bristol and Swansea via Newport, Cardiff and Port Talbot via the M4 motorway was introduced on 19th September 1981, run jointly by SWT, National Welsh and Bristol Omnibus. A special livery, with red and blue stripes running along the sides from the ExpressWest fleetname, is shown here on number 105 (LCY 105X), a Leyland Leopard PSU3F/4R with Willowbrook 003 Express 49-seat bodywork. It was one of eight similar vehicles delivered in plain white at the end of 1981 but given the ExpressWest livery to meet the demand of the route, which had begun using slightly older vehicles.

Six new 12-metre Leopards were also added to the fleet in 1982, these being PSU5E/4R models with Duple Dominant IV Express bodywork seating 53. Number 116 is seen in National Express livery.

Leyland Leopard models with Duple or Plaxton bodywork ranging from 1972 to 1980 deliveries, taken into the fleet were given numbers 147-158 and 186-196. However, a depot closure did result from this exercise as Brunswick also took the 25 buses hitherto from the former United Welsh Clarence Terrace depot, allowing the latter to close. On the other hand, the decision to close the National Welsh overhaul works at Ely, Cardiff brought more work to Ravenhill as National Welsh buses from depots at Aberdare, Bridgend and Barry were brought in for repair.

The more recent ex-National Travel (West) coaches brought a new development to SWT as they were 12-metre models based on the PSU5 version of the Leopard chassis. In the summer of 1982, new additions 111 to 116 for the SWT fleet were also of this type, or more precisely PSU5E/4, and the Duple Dominant IV bodywork seated 53—they were noteworthy in being accepted for the new bus grant by virtue of the degree of use on stage carriage service and are thought to have been the first 12-metre grant coaches within NBC.

The National Express Rapide network called for a higher-specification type of coach and, for the Swansea-London service, SWT placed five Leyland Tiger coaches with Duple Caribbean bodywork in service in 1983, after using hired vehicles for a year. The standard Tiger incorporated refinements such as air suspension and an engine more powerful than that of the Leopard, but these vehicles had the then recently introduced 260 bhp version of the TL11 engine. The bodywork seated 46 and incorporated refreshment and toilet facilities. The first vehicle, No. 117 (RCY 117Y), is seen in Victoria Coach Station, London, which had become quite cramped due to the general expansion of express services. In the lower picture, sister vehicle 118 (RCY 118Y) is seen leaving Swnasea bound for London. In 1985/6, these vehicles were re-registered, Nos. 117 and 118 becoming MKH 893A and 889A respectively.

Another new coach development was the hiring of two of the powerful and well-appointed MAN SR280 coaches from the Devon-based Trathens concern for a period beginning in April 1982 for a new high-speed service from Swansea to London (Victoria Coach Station). This took advantage of the M4 motorway to cover the run in an initial schedule time of 3 hours 35 minutes, later reduced to 3 hours 30 minutes and formed part of NBC's new Rapide network. In practice the vehicles originally allocated were frequently changed for other MAN or Volvo coaches from Trathens' main fleet as the need arose.

Numbered 505, this was at first regarded as experimental, but proved highly successful. It was planned to purchase two of the Dennis Falcon models with Perkins V8 engines developed at NBC's instigation as

Rapide coaches for the route but in the event the Trathens coaches continued to run until May 1983, when the first of five Leyland Tiger coaches with the recently introduced Duple Caribbean bodywork arrived for use on this service. Numbers 117-121, they have 46 seats with toilet and refreshment facilities to Rapide standard, and were fitted with 260 bhp versions of the TL11 engine. A further five similar coaches, 122-126, were delivered the following year, the last of these having been diverted after delivery to National Welsh, although it had not entered service and received a registration number in sequence with the rest of the batch.

By that date, quite a network of express services linked the South Wales area with other parts of Wales as well as England, with SWT involvement in most of them. The Trawscambria services intended to improve

communication between north and south Wales had been expanded and included the 701 route from Swansea to Rhyl via Aberyswyth, the X52 Dyfed Dragon being described as 'the fast service' from Swansea to Aberyswyth. Conventional express services linked Swansea with Birmingham/Hull and Manchester, the latter operated jointly with Yelloway, as well as London and the Expresswest services linked Swansea and places to the West such as Llanelli, Tenby, Haverfordwest and Carmarthen with Cardiff and Bristol, with the two-hourly X21 linking Llanelli and a number of smaller towns via the M4 to Cardiff. A second Rapide service, 506, linked Haverfordwest, Pembroke, Carmarthen, Neath and London, which the 505 had been extended to serve Llanelli and Gorseinon on some journeys.

On the bus side, the supply of new

vehicles came to a complete standstill as the numbers of passengers carried continued to fall. There were reports early in 1982 that a planned order for 30 Leyland Olympian double-deckers had been cancelled and the final batch of Bristol VRT buses delivered in 1980 were to remain the most modern double-deckers in the fleet until 1986.

Even so, there were apt to be circumstances producing vehicle shortages. One arose when West Glamorgan County Council decided that school traffic should be carried on stage carriage buses. To meet this, second-hand Bristol VRT buses were acquired towards the end of 1982. Two G-registered examples, older than any in the existing fleet came from the United Automobile Services fleet and although the ECW bodywork was basically similar, seating capacity was 70 and the engines were Gardner 6LX units, in most parts of the country the usual VRT power unit but new to SWT. Even older, and one of the first production batch of VRT models, was a vehicle that originally entered service

with Eastern Scottish in December 1968. This was an example of the 33ft.-long VRTLL6G with ECW body seating 83 as built, though reduced to 77 later in its life. It had formed part of the exchange of VRT models for Lodekka buses that had occurred in the early 'seventies, being operated by Eastern National.

Another source of second-hand Bristol VRT buses was West Midlands PTE, which was beginning to withdraw its fleet of VRT buses with Gardner engines and MCW bodywork to standard WMPTE style dating from 1973-4. Five were added to the fleet, originally numbered 900-4, noteworthy from a SWT viewpoint in being taller than other double-deckers then in the fleet, though the 14ft. 2in. height was in line with WMPTE's characteristic 'intermediate' level. They did not have power-assisted steering but this was fitted before entry into service by the Alder Valley workshops. Such work upgrading the specification of vehicles in SWT's fleet—another example was the fitting of retarders to some Leyland

National single-deckers and Bristol VR double-deckers—created their own shortages of vehicles available for service and caused more vehicles to be hired in.

With the arrival of both hired and purchased buses from other fleets, SWT's presence on the streets and roads of its territory took on a varied appearance. Further mid-seventies Leyland Nationals were taken into stock but the batch numbered 350-353 differed from others in the fleet in being of the short 10.3-metre class and seating 41—two came from East Kent and two from Maidstone & District.

Then towards the end of 1983, London Transport's large-scale withdrawal of its Daimler Fleetlines provided a major source of double-deckers at attractive cost. A total of eight, all with Leyland 680 engines and MCW-built bodywork, were acquired via Ensignbus, the dealer responsible for disposal which also converted them from their original form with centre doorway to 76-seat layout with front entrance only. They were numbered

The West Midlands PTE was selling off some of its Bristol VRT buses and five were added to the SWT fleet in addition to two purchased as driver training vehicles. The chassis were of the VRTSL2 type, with Gardner 6LX engine, and thus largely familiar but the 76-seat bodywork by MCW was to WMPTE standard pattern of the period. Application of standard NBC red livery altered its character somewhat, in particular making the radiator grille, almost invisible against the original dark blue, more prominent. Originally numbered 900 on arrival with SWT, NOB 424M is seen here after renumbering as 859, later in 1983.

(Below) A need for single-deckers in the 10 metre category was met by the purchase of two pairs of 10.3-metre 41-seat Leyland National buses, from East Kent and Maidstone & District respectively. Number 351 (GFN 551N), one of the ex-East Kent buses, emits the puff of smoke so characteristic of the Leyland 510-engined National as it sets off from the Quadrant Centre for Port Talbot.

851-858 and it was decided to create what might be called a non-ECW series of double deckers, for the ex-West Midlands VRT buses were renumbered 859-863 (the VRT models from other NBC companies taking numbers 902-904). This was done to enable these vehicles, higher than standard VR types, to be readily identified by crews. In 1984, another ex-London Fleetline arrived, becoming 864, but it was of particular interest in having been rebuilt not only with single door but as a convertible open-topper.

By this period NBC subsidiaries were able to reassert their individuality to some degree and a revised livery began to appear on coaches and dual-purpose vehicles of white with maroon waistbands, grey stripes and the pre-

The availability of ex-London Transport Daimler Fleetline double-deckers had its effect on SWT, like many other fleets. All the eight purchased in 1983 were Leyland-engined with MCW bodywork, the original centre exit doors being replaced by standard windows in the process of a rebuild carried out by

Ensignbus, as shown by number 852 (KUC 902P), on the left, below. The right-hand picture of 854 (KUC 935P) shows that the amidships staircase position was not altered. The original London Transport numbers of these vehicles were respectively DMS 1902 and DMS 1935.

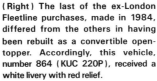

Some of the ex-London Fleetlines entered service in their existing livery, number 858 (KJD 19P) being in the style with upper-deck window surrounds in white which had been favoured by London Transport for a time beginning in the mid-1970s. Note also the prominent advertisement for the Swansea-Birmingham coach service.

(Right) The last of the ex-London Fleetline purchases, made in 1984, differed from the others in having been rebuilt as a convertible open-topper. Accordingly, this vehicle, number 864 (KUC 220P), received a white livery with red relief.

NBC style of fleetname. Meanwhile the economic pressure for further slimming continued with the miners' strike affecting not only the earnings of those who would have been working but also the whole community in the areas concerned. It cost SWT approximately £¾ million in lost revenue. In September 1984, Neath depot closed, though a small six-vehicle outstation was to continue. Until the 'sixties, there had been three bus depots in the town,

run by South Wales, Western Welsh and United Welsh respectively.

A change in operating needs saw the departure of the five short Bedford YMQS models with Lex 37-seat bodywork to Alder Valley in exchange for a pair of Bristol VRT with Gardner 6LXB engines, the latter becoming 996 and 997, an ironical event for the Bedfords had been the newest buses in the fleet, though a pair of Iveco 60-10 models with Robin Hood 19-seat

conversions to the van body shells numbered 72 and 73 on arrival early in 1985 injected new blood at the small end of the size range for coaching work.

The 1985 coach delivery of four more 260 bhp Leyland Tiger models with Duple 46-seat bodywork, this time of the latest Carribbean 2 design were numbered 127-130 and at first had matching registration numbers B127-130 CTH. However, a general policy of re-registering coaches, using numbers in

By 1985, major changes in both the style and substance of SWT's presence on the streets had begun to become apparent. The first new vehicles of overseas origin to be added to the fleet since the Saurer buses of 1926 and 1930 were a pair of mini coaches based on the Iveco 60-10 model, though the 19-seat conversion was carried out by Robin Hood. They carried the Flexibus fleetname, with neither the NBC emblem nor South Wales fleetname visible in this view.

From around 1982-83, NBC companies were encouraged to take a more independent line on matters of livery and display of fleetnames, for example. The South Wales version of the 'stripey' livery revived both the darker shade of red and a version of the South Wales fleetname lettering which was similar to that used up to the mid-1960s. It is seen here applied at the rear of one of the Willowbrook-bodied Leyland Leopard coaches, number 175 (BTH 483V). At this stage, the side panels had received the broad red band, plus the diagonal band just behind the front wheel arch, but not yet the grey stripes.

The full version of the 'stripey' livery is seen here applied to number 188 (LHU 661L), one of the vehicles transferred from the National Travel (South West) fleet in April 1981. It had been delivered new to the Bristol Omnibus Co Ltd in 1973 and was a Leyland Leopard PSU3B/4R with Plaxton Panorama Elite III 47-seat bodywork.

In 1985-86, the more modern South Wales coaches were re-registered in the MKH ...A series, some of the vehicles involved thus exchanging relatively up-to-date registrations for some that implied first licensing in 1963! Seen below with their new plates are numbers 123 (now MKH 82A, originally A123 XEP) and 120 (now MKH 831A, originally RCY 120Y), in both cases Leyland Tiger TRCTL11/3R with Duple Caribbean 46-seat bodywork.

The original registration numbers of the 1985 delivery of coaches were retained only for a year, but this photograph of number 128 as B128 CTH was taken during that period. The Leyland Tiger chassis with 260bhp TL11 engine was again favoured as was Duple Caribbean 46-seat bodywork, though the latter was of the Caribbean 2 type, with modified grille, etc. This vehicle became MKH 69A in 1986.

Re-registered after ten years service were the three Leyland Leopard coaches that had been transferred when new from Midland Red in 1976. Number 185 (now MKH 644A), the same vehicle illustrated as JOX 443P on page 73, also shows the National Holidays livery applied to vehicles largely used on such duties. The Plaxton Supreme bodywork was substantially as built but a Supreme IV grille and headlamps had modernised the appearance.

the MKH... A series was being adopted, applying to various vehicles ranging from M or N registered AEC Reliance models right up to the latest Tigers.

Extensive service cuts led to the withdrawal of the entire batch of twelve W-registered Bedford YMQ Duple-bodied buses plus various second-hand Leyland National and Bristol VRT buses in the autumn of 1985.

The first new double-deckers for five years arrived towards the end of 1985, seven Leyland Olympian models with ECW 75-seat bodywork and thus in some degree the obvious successor to the ECW-bodied Bristol VRT. However, they broke new ground in having Cummins L10 engines and Voith transmission. They were given the fleet numbers 901-907, the previous vehicles

occupying these numbers having been withdrawn or renumbered to fill gaps among later batches.

The Transport Act 1985 laid down that NBC subsidiaries were to be 'privatised' and, even before its passing, their character had been altering. The organisation of NBC had been revised and although for a time SWT had found itself in a vast 'Wales and the North' Region, the era of centralised control was ending. The other major feature of the 1985 Act effect on the bus industry was deregulation, meaning the opening up of services to competition. To prepare for this, the operating companies were investigating which routes could be operated without subsidy from public funds. This, in turn, enabled the management to evaluate

the possibilities of making a commercial success of the Company as a whole.

Mr D. J. R. Bending had been General Manager since 1980, and from 1984 combined this post with the General Managership of National Welsh. In 1986, the Government's requirement that companies be sold separately and that the relationship with NBC headquarters should be at 'arms length' in preparation for this, led to a change in organisation. Mr Bending was appointed Managing Director of SWT and he and his management team began to consider the possibilities of a management buy-out.

In common with many other NBC subsidiaries, the idea of running frequent minibuses on suitable urban

The final manifestation of NBC standards in new vehicle design and finish was the arrival in the latter part of 1985 of seven Leyland Olympian double-deckers with ECW 75-seat bodywork, outwardly very like those supplied to various other NBC subsidiaries from 1981 onwards. However, once again SWT broke unfamiliar ground with its choice of engine, for these were among the first supplied with the Cummins L10 unit of 10-litre capacity, although subsequently it was to become nominally the standard choice after Leyland Bus became an independent business. They also had Voith automatic transmission and accordingly the chassis designation was ONCL10/RV. The bodywork was to the low-height design developed as the successor to the version for the VRT chassis used by most NBC companies. The poppy red livery with the double-N emblem was soon to go out of favour too. They were numbered 901 upwards, a group of numbers which had been allocated to a succession of noteworthy double-deckers, number 903 (C903 FCY) being seen when new.

The square-cut rear styling of the ECW standard body for the Olympian is shown by this view of number 907.

services as a means of coping with the requirements of competitive operation had been considered. An initial batch of fifteen Mercedes-Benz L608D models with their van body shells converted as 20-seat buses by Robin Hood arrived early in 1986, for use on a new Swansea 'City Mini' network. They were numbered 201 upwards, thus re-interpreting the 'buses, small seating capacity' tag applied to this series of numbers from 1971. They also introduced a new livery of two-tone green, red and yellow, and the first route, appropriately from a historical viewpoint, was Swansea, Mumbles and Oystermouth, introduced in February 1986 thus echoing the original railway which began the South Wales story.

In the summer of 1986, SWT took delivery of four new coaches which illustrated the way in which vehicle policy no longer followed a centralised NBC pattern. Number 131 was a Duple integral 425 model with 49 seats, while the other three were examples of the Plaxton 4000 double-deck coach with 71-seat capacity based on Neoplan 722 six-wheeled underframe in this case with the 15-litre Gardner 6LYT engine. These were the first six-wheelers in the fleet since the pre-war AEC Renown models and entered service as numbers 151-153. Further deliveries of Mercedes-Benz L608D minibuses converted by Robin Hood comprised five with coach seats for nineteen passengers and 33 more 20-seat buses.

Noteworthy departures from the fleet in the summer of 1986 were the last AEC vehicles to remain in operational service with SWT, the three Reliance coaches with Duple Dominant bodywork, numbers 180-182 dating from 1974 and originally registered TCY 180M and UCY 181-182N but laterly 'disguised' as MKH 730A, 790A and 679A. Thus the AEC era at South Wales ended, having lasted for two-thirds of a century, equivalent to the period of

time AEC was producing vehicles though that had ended in 1979.

A new livery for full-sized buses appeared in the spring of 1987, again basically a two-tone green (lime and leaf) with yellow and red bands bordered in white. This represented a break with tradition in that South Wales buses had been painted in red as the principal or only colour since 1920, though using varying shades and with relief, usually in cream or white, to varying extent. However, green had been used in the Company's earliest days and, indeed, green had tended to be quite common on early BET-group motor buses.

On 8th May, 1987, The South Wales Transport Co Ltd was purchased by the management team led by David Bending, being the 35th NBC subsidiary to be sold in a process which had begun in July 1986 and was completed in April 1988. On the purchase date, there were 950 employees and 265 vehicles, the latter figure only a little less than the 285 operated in 1938, although of course that was long before the major amalgamation with United Welsh, etc of 1971 and the earlier and later absorbtion of various operators and parts of the former Western Welsh territory.

Later in 1987 a further 25 minibuses were added to the fleet for use in the West Swansea area, the choice this time falling on the integral MCW Metrorider.

The main event of the early part of 1988 was the acquisition of the business of A. E. & F. R. Brewer Ltd of Maesteg. This was another of the old-established independent operators whose vehicles were a familiar sight going back to the early days of the development of bus services, having been established by about 1921, originally in Caerau, the fleet having grown to eleven by 1935, the principal route linking Caerau and Maesteg.

Some 34 vehicles were in the fleet at the time of purchase, and eleven of these were on AEC Reliance chassis (indirectly reviving the SWT link with AEC) with five Leyland Leopard and one Tiger Cub, six Bedford, four DAF, two Dennis Lancet and among smaller vehicles, two Bristol LHS, a Ford A-series, a Mercedes-Benz L608D and the most recent purchase, an MCW Metrorider.

It is noteworthy, however, that the Brewer concern was not absorbed by SWT. At the time of the management buy-out, a company had been formed by the managment team, at that stage having the name Novel Cobra Ltd, its function being to act as the concern which was to acquire The South Wales Transport Co Ltd from NBC. Shortly after privatisation, the name of Novel Cobra Ltd was changed to United Welsh Services Ltd, reviving the historic name for the concern which was to be the holding company for not only SWT but also the Brewer business when taken over in January 1988 and then Llynfi Motor Services Ltd of Maesteg in July 1988. The latter was another old established business with seventeen vehicles, based on Leyland chassis apart from two Bristol LH6L. There were ten Leopard models of various types, mainly Plaxton-bodied coaches, four Atlantean double-deckers with Alexander bodywork and a Leyland Tiger Cub. This fleet was merged with that of the nearby Brewer business.

Then in December 1988, the Swansea operations of J. Cleverley Ltd of Cwmbran, which operated under the Capitol Coaches Group name, were acquired. Capitol had moved into the Swansea area by acquiring the business of Morris Bros. The consequence of these moves was the establishment of United Welsh Coaches, with vehicles from both the Capitol concern and others transferred from SWT.

The increasing variety of new vehicle intake for NBC subsidiaries in the final years of the group is indicated by the delivery of coaches to SWT in 1986. Number 131, which was registered as 999 BCY, was a Duple Integral 425 49-seat SDAK 1503 model. It was painted in National Holidays livery.

Three of the Plaxton Paramount 4000 double-deck coaches were purchased for the Rapide services. They seated 71 passengers and were based on the Neoplan 722 underframe with Gardner 6LYT engine. Number 152 (300 CUH) is shown here.

(Below) Lined up in the new liveries adopted in 1987 are number 242 (D242 LCY), one of the second batch of Mercedes-Benz L608D models with 19-seat conversions by Robin Hood; 773 (JTH 773P), a Leyland National; 168 (NCY 476R), a Leyland Leopard with Duple Dominant Express body, and 936 (TPE 152S), one of a pair of Bristol VRT with Gardner engines acquired from Alder Valley in 1984.

Competition and vehicle policy.

The mergers quoted in the preceding paragraphs are related to the experience of SWT and, following privatisation, the United Welsh group as it has developed. Although independent operators were still quite numerous, in the period up to 1986 SWT was involved in joint operation of a service with two independent operators (D Coaches and Rees & Williams) and four other such concerns ran in the west Glamorgan area. From deregulation in October 1986, there was an upsurge of independent bus operation, with ten routes on which SWT was faced with direct competition, but by December 1987 the competing services had vanished on all but two.

Among the more noteworthy were the operations of Cream Line in the Neath area and minibus operation by Jervis Bros and Margam Cabs in the Port Talbot area. Independent operators had tended to offer lower fares but subsequent withdrawals of services, and in some cases demise of the business, imply that costs were not being covered. Competition had tended to come in waves, with the first wave at the beginning of deregulation in October 1986, and a second in 1987, some of which was a reaction to the withdrawal of the earlier services. In 1988-89, a third wave has materialised, this time concentrated on areas west of Swansea.

South Wales Transport had introduced high-frequency minibuses in the Mumbles area eight months before deregulation in February 1986, the fleet growing quickly from the initial fifteen to 53 a year later and 88 by late 1987. They operate in the Swansea, Neath, Port Talbot and Llanelli areas, the type originally favoured being the Mercedes-Benz L608D, originally chosen largely because of its suitability for 20-seat bodywork, preferred to the 16-seat size for SWT's type of service. The MCW Metrorider was chosen for a batch of 25-seat vehicles but subsequent orders reverted to Mercedes-Benz after good experience with the earlier examples, the latest including five 811 models and 36 814 with 31-seat bodywork by Robin Hood.

The fleet up to 1985 had been standardised on Leyland group vehicles but the dismantling of the NBC organisation on privatisation broke the almost automatic connection between NBC subsidiaries and Leyland — the group discount on spares prices was not continued, for example. The Leyland National and Bristol VRT buses had proved expensive vehicles to operate, though the Leyland Tiger was better and the one batch of Leyland Olympian double-deckers with Cummins engines had proved very successful. It was planned to phase out the Leyland National and, indeed, no more full-sized single-decker bus purchases were planned, for frequent minibus services had shown an ability to generate more revenue from which the cost of running the larger fleet of minibuses could be met.

The double-deck fleet would be kept, though the number in use would probably drop to about 50. Some Bristol VR buses had been overhauled for use as a means of keeping fleet quality up, but some new double-deckers would probably be purchased in due course. Among coaches, the Duple Integral 425 had lived up to the claims of lower running costs than most other types and, though there had been teething troubles, was regarded as a probable choice for future coach orders.

Brewer's Motor Services, acquired by the new-generation United Welsh Services Ltd in 1988 and thus now a company associated with SWT, is another concern with a long history of favour for AEC vehicles. This AEC Regal III of the preselective gearbox 9621E type, with bodywork by Harrington, dated from 1949.

Llynfi Motor Services Ltd, on the other hand, had a long history of favouring Leyland chassis. This Tiger PS-model first registered early in 1950 is of interest as it had bodywork by Longford of Neath, one of several concerns with transport connections set up by Col. R. G. Llewellyn, Managing Director of Neath & Cardiff Luxury Coaches Ltd, which came into the SWT fold in 1971 as described on page 58.

David Bending, Managing Director of SWT puts the Company on NBC's privatisation map at the official hand-over on 8th May 1987. On the left of the picture is Alan Kreppel, Commercial Director, while on the right are Gerard Turley, Finance Director and Ivan Moore, Technical Director.

People

The people involved in any enterprise are almost literally its lifeblood. A largely pictorial record of SWT's 75-year history such as this does not allow space to do anything like adequate justice to those who contributed to the firm's success, over that lengthy period.

Despite the obvious sense of a new start with the privatisation of the Company, SWT has an atmosphere of continuity in regard to its management, workforce and, in many respects, the way things are done. 'Professional' is perhaps the word that comes to mind, and although operating very effectively in today's competitive environment, evidence that this is a concern maintaining high standards on the basis of sound experience is not hard to find.

The management buy-out team was led by David Bending, who had been appointed General Manager with effect from 1st May 1980, being appointed Managing Director when SWT was being prepared as a 'free standing' concern rather than one woven into the structure of the National Bus Company, as had applied previously. Prior to his appointment to SWT he had been Traffic Manager of Southdown Motor Services Ltd.'

Similarly, Alan Kreppel, Commercial Director, had been appointed Traffic Manager from 1st June 1982. The other members of the buy-out team who are Directors of the Company are Gerard Turley, Financial Director, and Ivan Moore, Technical Director. Mr Turley

quoted an instance of continuity in 'the Weedy formula', devised by Mr H. Weedy, General Manager 1955-64, which still provides the basis for people, absent for long periods due to illness, retaining the right to 'stay on the books' for re-employment if later restored to fitness.

However, others contributed significantly to the success of the new venture. Mr L. B. Beynon, Secretary from November 1965 to August 1988, though deciding against becoming a member of the buy-out was a major participant in preparing the Company for privatisation — his period of office had included the difficult days of the early and mid 1970s when having enough money to pay the wages was sometimes far from being assured. Peter Wood, Chief Engineer from 1962 to 1985, did much which contributed to the ability of the Company to maintain its fleet to a high standard. There was a tendancy for NBC operating companies to lose their central works, either by closure or hiving off to form separate organisations during the final years of the group, but this had been successfully resisted by SWT. The works did take on outside work, however, and has built up a good reputation.

Mention must also be made of the trade union relationship. Labour relations in the transport industry tend to hit the headlines only in times of trouble, yet a constructive attitude on

both management and union sides plays a major part in the efficient working of many companies. This has long been true within SWT and it is noteworthy that the structure operating in NBC days still continues, even though the old 'National Agreements' have long since been replaced by locally negotiated replacements more in tune with modern practice and current requirements. Each depot has a trade union branch, the chairman and secretary of which represent the branch on the Fleet Committee.

The present Fleet Chairman is David John, a driver based in Swansea who has been employed by SWT for 21 years and who has been elected to sit on the National Committee of the Transport and General Workers Union's Passenger Services Group. The Fleet Secretary is Dillwyn Davies, one of the longest-serving drivers based at Ammanford and formerly a James employee before that concern was taken over by SWT.

As on the management side, the former holders of senior positions in the union structure played their part in building the present set-up. Another ex-James driver, Islwyn Thomas became a full-time District Officer for the TGWU when SWT took over the James business and was frequently involved in the negotiations needed as SWT grappled with the varying problems of the 'seventies and early 'eighties. He recalled a wartime incident when, as driver of one of two James buses in

David John, Fleet Chairman

Dillwyn Davies, Fleet Secretary

Islwyn Thomas, former TGWU District Officer

Swansea during an air raid one evening it was decided to break normal rules by leaving early as bombs began to fall nearby. Buildings were well alight and two buses were subsequently reported as having ignored a traffic policeman's stop signal, the policeman describing them in 'orange' (roughly James' livery), but Islwyn was able to claim 'innocence' by saying that the James' vehicles in question were wartime grey, though they may well have looked orange in the glow of the fires. He has been succeeded as TGWU District Officer by Jim Hancock.

The Fleet Chairman prior to David John was Bob Ley, who had been Branch Chairman for the former United Welsh Services Company, and though retired in 1984, is an active member of the Government's Disabled Person Transport Advisory Committee. Tommy Lewis of Neath was local Branch Officer, later becoming Fleet

Bob Ley, former Fleet Chairman

Secretary, previous to Dillwyn Davies's appointment.

Another noteworthy personality within the company is Peter Harris, who won the national 1988 Bus Driver of the Year competition after some five years of qualifying for the finals. He beat 57 other top drivers from across Britain in the finals held in Blackpool.

Peter Harris, Bus Driver of the Year, 1988

General Managers

P. R. Blake*	3/32 to 6/49
W. M. Dravers	7/49 to 12/54
I. L. Gray	12/54 to 6/55
H. Weedy	7/55 to /64
J. H. Gilbert	10/64 to 1/68
F. A. J. Woodworth	2/68 to 8/73
R. Brookes	9/74 to 10/74
C. A. McNamara	9/73 to 2/75
P. Harmer	3/75 to 1/80
D. J. R. Bending §	2/80 to date

* P. R. Blake was Managing Director 10/39 to 6/49

§ D. J. R. Bending has been Managing Director since May 1986

Traffic Managers

T. G. Clabburn	c/35 to c/39
W. Mayes	to 8/50
S. Harris	9/50 to 3/53
E. C. Hill	6/53 to 4/69
B. M. Horner	12/68 to 3/73
S. Senior	5/73 to 9/78
G. Varley	12/78 to 4/82
A. D. Kreppel § §	6/82 to date

§ § A. D. Kreppel has been Commercial Director since May 1986

Secretary

J. G. Death	/26 to 6/46
A. H. Trembath	6/46 to 11/51
I. M. Smith	11/51 to 3/56
D. P. Drew	4/56 to 10/65
L. P. Beynon	11/65 to 8/88
G. Turley**	to date

** G. Turley is Finance Director

Chief Engineer

T. L. Henry	c/38
H. F. Mathew	c/39
J. A. Parknell	to 6/46
L. M. Parker	8/46 to 10/55
P. C. Wickens	1/56 to 1/62
P. Wood	2/62 to 11/88
I. H. Moore § § §	12/85 to date

§ § § I. H. Moore has been Technical Director since May 1986

The Russell Street offices, seen here as they appeared in 1950, were for many years the Company's headquarters. The site, which also encompassed Brunswick Garage, had been acquired in 1914 and the original SWT fleet was housed here. The head office soon moved from Rutland Street and the office block was extended as the concern grew. These premises were demolished in 1963 to make way for the new offices shown below.

Premises

The new Russell Street offices came into use in April 1964, continuing until the headquarters moved to the present site in Heol Gwyrosydd, adjoining Ravenhill Works, in 1985.

Brunswick Garage in 1950, with 1949 AEC Regal III single-deckers and 1939 Leyland Titan TD5 double-deckers in evidence, though a pair of AEC Regent models are to be seen to the right of the centre pillar.

Ravenhill Works was built in 1937, arising from the major expansion of SWT's fleet needed to replace the Swansea tramway system. This view dates from 1950.

The body shop at Ravenhill in 1950. Many of the 1937 batch of AEC buses purchased to replace the trams were in course of extensive rebuild of their Weymann bodywork. Number 247 (ACY 46) remained in passenger service until 1956 when it became a training bus.

A campaign to improve the appearance of the fleet by rectifying minor accident damage resulted in this crowded scene in the Ravenhill body shop in 1953, with AEC Regal and Regent buses of various types under repair.

(Above) The Brecon Road garage at Pontardawe was built in 1928. This view, with 1948 lowbridge Regent No. 295, dates from 1950. The premises had become too small when replaced in 1960.

(Top, right) Eastland Road garage, Neath, was built on premises acquired on Christmas Day, 1933! It replaced an earlier smaller garage in London Road, but rationalisation in 1972 after the local United Welsh and Western Welsh premises were acquired led to concentration on the ex-WW depot.

(Right) Expansion of the Llanelly District Traction premises at Robinson Street, Llanelli became possible when the freehold was purchased from the electricity board in 1965. SWT's premises in Copperwork Road were then closed. Note the AEC Regent single-deckers.

(Below right) Haverfordwest garage was transferred from Western Welsh in March 1972, this view showing it in March 1969.

(Below) Ammanford garage, acquired with the James concern in 1962 was rebuilt as shown in 1968. An ex-James Leyland Tiger Cub emerges.

(Bottom right) Clarence Terrace had been the United Welsh depot in Swansea, coming into SWT ownership in 1971. It closed in April 1981.

South Wales Transport scene, 1989

(Above, left)
A batch of 25 MCW Metrorider models with 25-seat bodywork was added to SWT's fleet in 1987 for services in West Swansea. Number 259 (E259 REP) is seen in company with No.221, one of the earlier Mercedes-Benz L608D, the latter carrying roof advertising boards. The neat styling of the Metrorider is clearly apparent.

Recent additions to the minibus fleet have reverted to Mercedes-Benz and the upper right hand view shows No. 326, F326 DCY, with its square 25-seat bodywork by Reeve Burgess.

(Left)
A familiar name has been revived by the appearance of vehicles in the livery of United Welsh Coaches, in this case represented by U148 (JWE 248W), a Leyland Leopard PSU5 with Plaxton Supreme body. This further splash of colour enhances liveries to be seen in south Wales.

Acknowledgements

When this book was in the planning stage, I looked forward to what was bound to be a fascinating project. I know SWT well, in terms of the remarkable variety of vehicles operated over the years. Yet most of my knowledge was gathered from afar and clearly I was going to need a great deal of local expertise.

Chris Taylor is renowned for his knowledge of the bus industry as a whole and the part of it based in South Wales in particular. His contribution in providing the background information which explains why SWT followed its often unusual path has been invaluable — though I must own up to the responsibility for most of the words, many of the most interesting items stem from Chris's information.

Equally indispensible in a different dimension has been the support of the Company. The management team which took over SWT on privatisation have all helped — David Bending, for his overall approval of the project; Alan Kreppel, for allowing me access to the Company's archive material in which he takes a personal interest as well as providing a valuable picture of how the Company operates and its ideas for the future, plus Gerard Turley and Ivan Moore, for their respective help, both personal and in making items available. Special mention must be made of Phil Trotter, SWT's Marketing Officer, who not only acted in a liaison capacity but lent his remarkable personal collection of SWT vehicle photographs, the largest single source of illustrations, although many came from SWT itself and also from Chris Taylor's wide-ranging collection.

Other suppliers of photographs are listed in the Photocredits list, but mention must also be made of Mike Sutcliffe and Royston Morgan, who lent some of the official Brush photographs. The colour illustration used on the cover was provided by Roy Marshall.

Finally, I must thank the staff at TPC, Glossop, for their unfailing support in coping with my handwritten copy material and in keeping the wheels turning.